DATE DUE

# The Black
# Anti-Semitism
# Controversy

# The Black
# Anti-Semitism
# Controversy

## Protestant Views and Perspectives

Hubert G. Locke

SUP

Selinsgrove: Susquehanna University Press
London and Toronto: Associated University Presses

Associated University Presses
440 Forsgate Drive
Cranbury, NJ 08512

Associated University Presses
25 Sicilian Avenue
London WC1A 2QH, England

Associated University Presses
P.O. Box 338, Port Credit
Mississauga, Ontario
Canada L5G 4L8

The paper used in this publication meets the requirements of the American National Standard for Permanence of Paper for Printed Library Materials Z39.48-1984.

**Library of Congress Cataloging-in-Publication Data**

Locke, Hubert G.
    The black anti-semitism controversy: Protestant views and perspectives / Hubert G. Locke.
        p.   cm.
    Includes bibliographical references and index.
    ISBN 0-945636-51-2
    1. Antisemitism—United States.   2. Afro-Americans—Relations with Jews.   3. Christianity and antisemitism.   4. Afro-American churches. 5. United States—Ethnic relations.   I. Title.
    DS146.U6L63   1994
    305.8'00973—dc20

                                                    92-50999
                                                    CIP

PRINTED IN THE UNITED STATES OF AMERICA

# Contents

# Foreword

## FRANKLIN H. LITTELL

The present study of anti-semitism in the Black churches upsets some opinions that have gained credence in academic circles, as well as opinions that circulate widely in the public forum.

In this respect the study headed by Professor Locke is like the classic study produced more than a quarter of a century ago by Dr. Bernhard Olson: *Faith and Prejudice* (Yale University Press, 1961). Dr. Olson was a key figure in research and education for the major part of his life. During his most productive years he was on the staff of the National Council of Churches and the National Conference of Christians and Jews. He was also a friend and associate of Professor Locke in combating anti-semitism, during the last fifteen years of his life of research, writing, and teaching.

Dr. Olson's study concentrated upon materials used for the most part in white Protestant churches. By studying large quantities of primary sources, he established that some common assumptions about anti-semitism in white liberal and conservative Protestant circles were wrong.

Dr. Locke's study combines a comprehensive analysis of articles on Black anti-semitism with several in-depth surveys of Black congregations. He also comes to conclusions that challenge some received dogmas.

The most prominent and generally unquestioned academic dogma about anti-semitism is this: that intensity of religious commitment is predictive of intolerance, prejudice, and bigotry. (Behind this dogma is the hidden assumption that anti-semitism may be adequately treated as a form of "prejudice.") The dogma derives, of course, from the experience of enlightened men and women of the university when they try to communicate with minds still comfortably set in the pre-Enlightenment world. All too often anti-semitism, as well as other forms of bigoted stereo-typing, was a part of the worldview that prevailed in Christendom until modernity undermined the former stasis.

The reactions to "unenlightened" and "superstitious" attitudes in time became dogmas in their own right. The frozen orthodoxy of an earlier era was replaced first by the excitement of openness to new ideas and then by an orthodoxy of openness. Often forgot-ten was the truth that toleration of persons may be a virtue, but toleration of wrong-headed ideas is often an evil. The open and enlightened world of the modern universities and liberal politics proved utterly impotent when confronted by a terrorist movement like the NSDAP, a movement whose genocidal proclivities oc-cupied the centers of power in the German Third Reich.

Those who rallied internal German resistance to Nazism in the churches, such as the Confessing Church *(Bekennende Kirche)*, were not those whose minds were caves of all the winds of doctrine. Indeed, the collaborators *(Deutsche Christen)* attacked the resisters as "fundamentalists" precisely because they stubbornly held fast to certain traditional teachings that collided with the idolatry of the dictatorship *(Führerstaat)*. The collaborators, on the other hand—those churchmen who compromised and waffled in both teaching and action—were with but few exceptions avowed lib-erals. Article 24 of the Nazi Party Platform, never changed or modified since its adoption in 1920, announced and explained their religious open-door policy.

Professor Locke, having been a leading figure for many years in study and publication on the German Church Struggle *(Kir-chenkampf)* and the Holocaust *(Shoah)*, was free of the notion that religious commitment is *in itself* a negative. Neither was he chained to the common campus notion that openness to all ideas and programs that call themselves "modern" and "scientific" is *in itself* an affirmative quality in critical study. Freedom from these two crippling assumptions is particularly important in approaching sympathetically any study of the Black community, where conser-vative biblical Protestantism has been a major force for genera-tions.

The Locke study is free, therefore, of both the old pre-Enlight-enment dogmas and the dogmas of modernity. The study com-bines in a creative way the dialectic of empathy and analysis.

As might be expected in any report that is true to life, some of the results are ambiguous: some point to questions that need continuing attention and further in-depth research, rather than laying down axioms that may be taken as final for years to come. Other results point to reasonably firm hypotheses, ready to be thrown into the continuing debate about the nature of anti-semitism.

Black Protestantism has been theologically conservative and oriented to the Bible. Especially important: Black Protestantism is derived from the Radical Reformation rather than from the magisterial Reformers. There are few Black Christians in America in churches that were once state churches in colonial America and/ or Europe. Although the percentage of Black church members has for decades been approximately the same as the percentage of white church members, among the Black there are few Episcopalians, Lutherans, Evangelical and Reformed (*Unierte,* in the old country), Presbyterians, Congregationalists or—until recently— Roman Catholics. Four out of five have been Baptists, stemming from the Left Wing of the Reformation and especially from the Puritan line.

The churches of the Radical Reformation typically emphasize re-enactment, recapitulation, and restitution as central motifs, discontinuity rather than continuity, egalitarian democracy rather than hierarchical authority. The Bible and the Early Church have been the normative references.

The names of local Black congregations frequently show the theme of the restitution of the Early Church: "First Corinthian Church," "Galilee Missionary Church," "Bethel," "New Testament Church," and so on. Until recently, both male and female babies frequently were given Biblical names. Coming from the tradition of radical Puritanism, the Black Baptists have traditionally been Judaeophile rather than hostile to the Jewish people. The re-enactment of the Exodus has been one of the constant themes of Black preaching.

Dr. Locke points out that although the religious factor has been primary in the Black community, in discussions of Black anti-semitism the authors' presuppositions have generally made the economic factor primary. But even if the economic factor be made dominant, surveys of Blacks show that the Jews share in the general hostility felt by the city dwellers against their white exploit-ers—but come off better than other whites when distinctions are made between white elements.

The perception of Black anti-semitism has also been gravely skewed by the media's lust for the sensational and also by the Jewish community's anxieties about any resurgence of the hostility for which they paid so heavily a half century ago. Individuals who do not reject association with anti-semites (e.g., Jesse Jackson) or others who espouse overtly some of anti-semitism's most objec-tionable features (e.g., Louis Farrakhan) tend—by media sensa-tionalism on the one hand and Jewish anxiety on the other—to be taken for more representative of the Black churches' attitude to the Jews than they really are.

The study is necessarily oriented toward modern anti-semit-ism—that is, toward overt expressions of active prejudice, fre-quently exploited for political reasons. But beneath modern anti-semitism, which is just over a century old, there are layers of theological and cultural anti-semitism that are centuries old. Black Christians are rather less burdened than whites at these first and second levels of anti-semitism, which have been traditional in Christendom for a millennium and a half.

Theological anti-semitism, going back to the time of the system-atic rejection of the Jews and the Jewish heritage by the imperial Gentile church, has been modified in Black preaching and teach-ing by Black identification with the people of the Exodus and the people of the Early Church—two identities often elided by a peo-ple dependent upon oral tradition more than historical docu-ments. In general it may be said that theological anti-semitism has been less corruptive to Black Christianity than to the white churches.

So too with the *cultural* anti-semitism so prominent in European society, both in Christendom before the Enlightenment and in many intellectual circles afterward. The Black Christians, already committed to the restoration of what they thought of as the Bibli-cal religion of the Early Church, have had neither religious nor cultural reasons to identify with the Latin Church of the Middle Ages, the state churches of the Protestant Reformation, or the elitism of the *Encyclopaedists*.

In the matter of anti-semitism of the modern type—the use of anti-semitism as a deliberate political weapon—there are more suggestive parallels between the white and Black churches. White populism has produced anti-semitism in the style of Henry Ford and Tom Watson; Black populism has produced a *völkisch* movement in Black Islam. Anti-Zionism—the barely disguised anti-semitism of anti-Israel vehemence—has found lodging in both Black and white Christian circles. But in both cases the proponents of open anti-semitism, whether conscious or unwitting, are still distinctly in the minority. In white Protestantism they are far less influential then they were when Gerald L. K. Smith, Henry Ford, and Gerald Winrod were reaching tens of millions by radio who—combined with the following of Father Coughlin on the Roman Catholic side—were a major force in American internal and international policies.

The most disturbing fact uncovered by the Locke study concerns evidence that the younger generation of America Blacks, including those better educated, shows more indications of anti-semitism than did the generations of their parents and grandparents. This must be correlated with another development not treated in this study: the shift of able young Blacks away from church careers. The church was once the chief channel to leadership in the Black community. The opening up of the doors of opportunity in law, medicine, sports, business, and elsewhere has resulted in a marked shift of attention away from the church and its concerns.

During the most tense years of the civil rights struggle, the high quality of the Black clergy and the leadership they gave their people in nonviolent direct action was an invaluable countervailing force to those who wanted to respond to white violence in kind. Only at the time of the assassination of Martin Luther King, Jr. did the moral direction break down temporarily, giving the country a sudden glimpse of what the whole scene might have been like but for the authority of the Black churches, their pastors, and lay leaders.

For at least three generations the Black churches have had a great deal more influence over their members than have the mainline white churches. If in fact the churches are losing their influence with the younger Blacks, a matter urgently requiring further and extensive investigation in depth, the consequences can be most ominous for the American republic. A rise of anti-semitism will then by no means be the only danger sign, although such a development is certainly one of the most critical of warning signals.

The Locke study makes clear that if such a thing should happen it will mark a radical break from the preaching, teaching, and attitudes that have thus far characterized the Black churches in America.

# Introduction

> When we speak in abstract terms of the tension between individual liberty and equality or between individual liberty and social justice, we are apt to forget that fights do not occur between abstract ideas. These are not struggles between individuals as such and society as such, but between groups of individuals in society, each group striving to promote social policies favorable to it and to frustrate social policies inimical to it. (Carr 1961, pp. 40–41)

The essays in this volume seek to unravel and place in perspective one of the most contentious issues in contemporary American society. Essentially, the controversy swirls around whether and to what extent Black Americans manifest discernible traits of anti-semitism in their attitudes toward and relationships with Jewish people. As every analysis of any issue confronts at the outset a problem of bias or the angle of vision of the analyst-observer, it is best to state that which underlies this study.

The central portion of these essays contains the findings from a survey of Black Protestants in three American cities regarding their attitudes toward Jewish people. Conducted by a nationally distinguished social scientist, this portion of the study stands or falls on its own methodological merits. It should be weighed in the context of an extensive literature on the topic of Black anti-semitism that has been published over the past four decades.

The remainder of the essays attempt to provide a background and assessment of the issue of Black anti-semitism as it has been discussed and debated for at least the past half century in American society. The analysis draws heavily on a chronological description of viewpoints expressed in books, articles, monographs, and other statements, focusing particularly on the period since World War II.

Chronologies are the stuff of which histories are written; it is important, therefore, to disavow any intent on the part of the author to write a history of the controversy over Black anti-semitism. In Jefferson's words, "a decent respect for the opinions"—in this instance, of historians—precludes any such claim. The essays, however, attempt to follow the historian's approach to his or her craft, as expressed by E. H. Carr:

> . . . a provisional selection of facts and a provisional interpretation in the light of which that selection has been made—by others as well as by himself. . . . both the interpretation and the selection and ordering of facts undergo subtle and perhaps partially unconscious changes through the reciprocal action of one on the other . . . an unending dialogue between the present and the past. (1961, p. 35)

# I

Nearly any year in the past half-century would provide a window on the debate that has surged between Black and Jewish protagonists over the issue of Black anti-semitism in America. 1948, however, saw the occurrence of two events—one major, the other minuscule—which, in the light of subsequent occurrences, have proven to be pivotal both for those who affirm the existence of Black anti-semitism and for those who question, if not deny, its existence.

The major event was the establishment of the State of Israel. That same year, the celebrated Black writer, James Baldwin, wrote an essay that appeared in the Winter issue of one of the principal American Jewish journals and that reflected Baldwin's musings about what he termed ". . . the Negro's ambivalent relation to the Jew." Speaking of the Black sermons, which he heard endlessly as a youth, Baldwin wrote:

> To begin with, though the traditional accusation that the Jews killed Christ is neither questioned or doubted, the term "Jew" actually operates in this initial context to include all infidels of white skin who have failed to accept the Savior. No real distinction is made: the preacher begins by accusing the Jews of having refused the light and proceeds from there to a catalog of their subsequent sins and the sufferings visited on them by a wrathful God. Though the notion of the suffering is based on the image of the wandering, exiled Jew, the context changes unperceptively to become a fairly obvious reminder of the trials of the Negro, while the sins recounted are the sins of the American republic.
>
> At this point, the Negro identifies himself almost wholly with the

Jew. . . . The hymns, the texts, and the most favored legends are all Old Testament and therefore Jewish in origin: the flight from Egypt, the Hebrew children in the fiery furnace, the terrible jubilee songs of deliverance. . . . The covenant God made in the beginning with Abraham and which was to be extended to his children and his children's children forever is a covenant made with these Latter-day exiles also; as Israel was chosen, so are they.

The birth and death of Jesus . . . also implements this identification. . . . it was Jesus who made it possible, who made salvation free to all, "to the Jew first and afterwards to the Gentile." The image of the suffering Christ and the suffering Jew are wedded with the image of the suffering slave, and they are one. . . .

But this same identification, which Negroes, since slavery, have accepted with their mother's milk, serves, in contemporary actuality, to implement an involved and specific bitterness. Jews in Harlem are small tradesmen, rent collectors, real estate agents and pawnbrokers; they operate in accordance with the American business tradition of exploiting Negroes, and they are therefore, identified with oppression and are hated for it. . . .

The Negro, facing a Jew, hates, at bottom, not his Jewishness, but the color of his skin. It is not the Jewish tradition by which he has been betrayed but the tradition of his native land. But just as society must have a scapegoat, so hatred must have a symbol. Georgia has the Negro and Harlem has the Jew.[1]

## II

Baldwin's essay has had a profound impact on the character, course, and content of the debate over Black anti-semitism ever since it appeared. It has entered the mainstream of the literature on the debate where it is quoted almost canonically as a prooftext whenever observers of Black anti-semitism wish to cite an authoritative source. It provided a set of personal recollections that became cases-in-point for the theory on which social scientists were already at work: that economic contacts and relationships between Black and Jewish Americans lie at the base of Black hostility toward Jewish people. And in its "Georgia has the Negro and Harlem has the Jew" summation, Baldwin's commentary launched a trend of elevating to national significance events that transpired between Black and Jewish Americans in New York City.

Ironically, Baldwin wrote his essay as a protest against a series of anti-Jewish articles that appeared in the *Liberator,* an American

Black Nationalist publication founded after World War I. Baldwin was a member of the *Liberator's* editorial board and his article of protest, which appeared in the Jewish publication, *Commentary*, accompanied his resignation from the board. Ironically also, little subsequent attention has been devoted to Baldwin's incisive description of the content of Black preaching in relation to the Jewish Biblical tradition and the subtle but powerful manner in which that tradition is translated and incorporated into a reinterpretation of the Black experience in America.

Instead, it is the idea of economics as the root of the problem between Black and Jewish people in America, together with the perception that Black attitudes that result from such economic relationships constitute a form of anti-semitism that has come to dominate the debate on this issue. The persistence of this viewpoint will be seen in the discussion and analysis of the literature throughout this volume.

A description of this viewpoint, however, should not be confused with a defense of its validity. It would be a serious error, in fact, to read this volume as an attempt to displace the notion of Black anti-semitism with an ostensibly more benign and justifiable view of Black anti-Jewishness based on economic relationships. Prejudice, whatever its source, is a dangerous malady; Black and Jewish people especially have more than ample reason to recognize and understand this fact.

Nevertheless, in the instance of anti-Jewish biases, identifying such and determining their sources does not resolve the issue of anti-semitism, except for those for whom any expression of bias toward Jewish people is properly labeled "anti-semitic." For most observers, as noted in the first essay in this volume, anti-semitism-as-prejudice cuts too wide a definitional swath. The classical definitions of prejudice, such as those provided by Gordon Allport, picture it as "thinking ill of others without sufficient warrant" or "a feeling, favorable or unfavorable, toward a person or thing, prior to, or not based on, actual experience" or "an assertive or hostile attitude toward a person who belongs to a group simply because (he/she) belongs to that group, and is therefore presumed to have the objectionable qualities ascribed to the group" (1954).

Such attitudes, thoughts, or feelings, when directed toward Jewish persons, may well be a precondition of anti-semitism and, as such, dangerous in their own right. Tragically, however, history is sufficiently replete with specific examples of overt violent acts toward Jewish people to give us a defining quality of anti-semitism that far exceeds the boundaries of "thinking ill without sufficient warrant" and "assertive or hostile attitudes." Pogroms against Jewish communities throughout the Middle Ages serve to suggest a unique dimension of anti-semitism; the virtual destruction of European Jewry under the aegis of the German Third Reich provides a modern and ultimate example of its particular virulence and outcome.

It is the Holocaust, undoubtedly, which gives every Jewish person reason to fear any manifestation of prejudice toward Jewish people. But it is precisely the Holocaust that requires we make every effort to analyze and understand what is and is not anti-semitism. To inquire into the Holocaust is to examine a sequence of events that led to the formation and implementation of a government policy designed to exterminate Jewish people throughout Europe and—if the Nazis had been successful in their larger aims of conquest—throughout the Western world. It is at least arguable that the attitudes, feelings, and sentiments that drove that policy and its implementation are different substantively, in kind and quality, from those that permit one to "think ill of others without sufficient warrant."

If so, the question of whether prejudicial feelings may escalate to the level or anti-semitic beliefs and behavior becomes crucial. Put in a contemporary context and acknowledging the prejudice that exists against Jewish people in American society, would that prejudice combine, under certain circumstances, with the known pockets of virulent anti-semitism in this nation to produce pogroms or a policy of genocide against the American Jewish populace? It is a question the importance of which begs for an answer. Unfortunately, we have only assertions to guide us. One assertion would hold that the values, principles, structures, and experience of American democracy would not permit such events to occur. The other is the insight we gain from Hannah Arendt: that a potential once realized becomes within the range of human behavior forever.

Whatever the answer, Black as well as Jewish Americans have a particular stake in the question. If there are large pockets of prejudice in American society that parallel those directed toward the Jewish people, they are directed toward Black Americans as well. The possible fate of Jewish people in America or in any other society in which they are a minority, therefore, ought to be of especial concern to Black citizens, wherever they find themselves in similar circumstances. The experiences of any minority group is never far from the potential experiences of all other minorities in any society.

## III

This study is part of a series of inquiries commissioned by the Vidal Sassoon International Center for the Study of Anti-semitism at the Hebrew University of Jerusalem. Grateful appreciation is expressed to the center's director, Professor Yehuda Bauer, for his organization of an international effort to assess the contemporary features of this age-old problem and for inviting the authors of this study to participate. Equal gratitude is expressed to Professor Franklin H. Littell, the venerable Dean of Holocaust Studies among American scholars and, since its inception, chairman of the board of the William O. Douglas Institute, who, among his endless commitments to Jewish-Christian relations, guided the initiation of a comprehensive set of inquiries in the United States on the religious dimensions of this issue, which are also being supported by the Vidal Sassoon Center.

A survey such as this is the work of many individuals. The survey research was fielded in Buffalo by Ms. Karen McCadden, research assistant to Professor Raymond G. Hunt; in St. Louis by students of Professor Harry James Cargas, one of the principal Catholic scholars on the Holocaust; and in Seattle by Ms. Collette Carter, a Ph.D. candidate at the University of Washington. The exhaustive review of the literature was undertaken by Dr. Warren Lewis, whose scholarly skills are amply displayed in the annotation of the major works written on the topic since World War II. Especial appreciation is extended to the respondents to this survey for their generous cooperation and to the pastors of their churches, without whose assistance in arranging for the distribution of the questionnaires after Sunday morning services or during other weekly church activities, the survey would not have been possible.

Finally, the William O. Douglas Institute, which first proposed this study and is responsible for its conduct, has to its credit almost two decades of inquiries and research related to problems of race and ethnicity in American life. This period and the accompanying effort has resulted not only in a number of fruitful research collaborations but also in firm friendships, of which this study is one of many reflections. Raymond Hunt, Professor of Management and Organizations at the State University of New York at Buffalo and former Director of its Survey Research Center, is Senior Fellow and Director of Research of the Douglas Institute. Lyman H. Legters, Professor of Russian and East European History at the University of Washington is Senior Fellow of the Institute and its Director of Publications. Throughout this study, Hunt's unfailing good humor and his devotion to the rigors of data analysis guided the effort through many a frustrating moment, while Legters provided that rare blend of support and helpful criticism that helps to make otherwise conventional academic research relevant and readable to a wider audience.

## Author's Postscript

Discerning readers will discover that the debate on Black anti-semitism is reflected even in the perspectives of the several contributors to this volume. Professor Legters, in his exploration of the "rational explanatory value" of some manifestations of anti-semitism, discusses an important historical analogue in nineteenth-century eastern Europe and concludes that there is something properly called Black anti-semitism that is at least partially explicable as a primitive response to oppression. I have taken a narrower view, based largely on an analysis of the empirical studies on the topic and on the distortions to which the term "Black anti-semitism" lends itself and, accordingly, reject it as invalid.

Rather than attempting to gloss over or smooth out these differences or—perhaps to some even more important—to reconcile them in the text, I have chosen to let them stand as examples of the liveliness of the controversy on this issue that occurs, even between colleagues who share similar values, and as an expression of the importance that scholars attach to free, open, and unfettered inquiry.

# The Black
# Anti-Semitism
# Controversy

# 1
## The Problem Stated

Centuries of unrestrained antipathy toward their culture, religion, and role in Western societies—in some instances, even their existence—have made the Jewish people understandably concerned about any display of anti-Jewishness, in whatever form or circumstances it might occur. The virtual destruction of European Jewry, undertaken by a nation-state that represented a veritable paradigm of Western society and culture, has provided a grim warning to Jews and non-Jews alike regarding the ultimate outcomes to which anti-Jewish sentiments may lead. It is not surprising, therefore, that hostility toward Jews from any source should be viewed with particular alarm among Jewish people.

Such expressions, for the past century, have come to be depicted under the term "anti-semitism".[1] In contemporary usage, the term embraces a wide variety of attitudes and behaviors, ranging from offensive stories in which Jewish people are stereotyped characters to the Nazi-inspired Holocaust. It is the widespread currency of the term and the breadth of its application that pose one of the central problems of this study.

In contrast to popular usage, scholars have sought to define the phenomenon of anti-semitism in more precise and constrained terms. Their efforts have not been uniform nor consensual, resulting in depictions that encompass "inflexible judgment, almost always finding its outlet in discriminatory action" (Glock and Siegelman 1969, p. VI) to specific and manifest "Jew-hatred." (Bauer 1978, p. 8 Fn.) While it also lacks the precision and specificty one might prefer, the latter term conveys the underlying sentiment that is at issue and, therefore, is the meaning of anti-semitism that underlies this inquiry.

Either the broad-gauged definition of prejudice seeking an outlet in discriminatory behavior or the more specific terminology

23

of "Jew-hatred" requires an effort to locate particular forms and manifestations of animosity against Jewish people toward one end of the scale or the other. This study, concerning the attitudes of American Black Protestants toward Jewish people, requires both a specification of those attitudes and their placement within the range of possible anti-Jewish sentiments.

In principle, the broad definition of anti-semitism-as-prejudice, if not workable as a general proposition, would be specifically inappropriate for this study, as it requires an ". . . outlet in discriminatory behavior." There may be significance in the fact that this definition is advanced by sociologists who are accustomed to thinking about group conflict in majority-minority terms and, in this instance, view Jewish people as a minority against whom the majority in a given society may manifest both inflexible judgments and discriminatory behavior. Black Protestants, however, are also a minority in American society; their capacity to display discriminatory behavior against Jewish people is minimal to nonexistent.

Nevertheless, American Black Protestants along with any other non-Jewish segment of the American populace are capable of manifesting "Jew-hatred" or, if one prefers a milder term, an undifferentiated antipathy toward Jews as individuals or as a group. The extent to which this manifestation is a reality, in contrast to an assumption, is the primary interest and focus of this study.

# I

As members of discernible minority groups in American society, both Black and Jewish Americans have been and are the recipients of prejudice and discrimination. On the Black American side of the ledger, the record runs from the history of slavery to more than a century of segregation in public schools, housing, employment, and places of public accommodation that persisted after the slave era had ended. Even today, residual negative majority attitudes toward Black Americans remain; where they do not appear in overt form, they occasionally find expression in such contemporary phrases as the "American underclass."[2] Jewish Americans likewise, have faced a persistent history of prejudice and discrimination in America, ranging from the recently abandoned practice of setting quotas for the admission of Jewish applicants to colleges, universities, and professional schools to the disbarment of Jews from participation in the more elite circles of the majority society. Both Black and Jewish Americans have experienced the extreme forms of animosity in America—lynching in the first instance and mob violence in the second—simply because of their discernible differences from the majority populace in the United States.

Given the historic Jewish concern with issues of social justice, traceable to Biblical times, and the common experience of Jewish and Black Americans with rejection by the larger American populace, it also is not surprising to discover the emergence of a common set of interests between the two groups. Shortly after the turn of the present century, this mutuality of interests became visible in the formation of the National Association for the Advancement of Colored People, several decades later in the rise of the nonskilled union movement, and in the general alignment of Black and Jewish Americans on issues of civil rights, civil liberties, and urban reform.[3]

It was this alignment of interests and the initiation of organizational mechanisms to advance them that ushered in the era of what has come to be known as the Grand Alliance[4]—the joint effort of primarily Black and Jewish Americans to bring about an end to discrimination and inequality in American society—overtly in the case of America's Black populace and more subtly and insidiously for its Jewish citizens. This joining of interests between two minority groups in America—the one, potentially powerful because of its numbers; the other, because of its intellectual and philanthropic resources—provided a stimulus for much of the social reform of the past half-century. Politically, it came to represent two major constituencies in the electoral base that produced the New Deal era.

It would be a mistake, however, to interpret the era of the Grand Alliance as a joining of efforts between Black and Jewish Americans, per se. All that can be said reliably is that the alliance represented a merging of interests between Black and Jewish leaders. Even relationships between the latter did not always follow a smooth, unruffled course, but they were sufficiently consistent and persistent to permit a description of the period between the founding of the NAACP (1909) and the death of Martin Luther King, Jr. (1968) as the era of mutually organized and expressed interests of leaders of the Black and Jewish communities on issues of social justice in America.

Whether the sentiments of Black and Jewish leaders during this era found support among the rank-and-file of either or both communities has never been determined. So pervasive, however, has the Grand Alliance been—both as ideal and as reality—that its breakdown after the assassination of Martin Luther King, Jr., while in actuality a breach between Black and Jewish leaders, was seen as a larger collapse in relationships between Black and Jewish Americans, acompanied by a dramatic increase, in the view of many Jewish observers, of distinctly anti-semitic attitudes among the Black populace.

## II

The breach between Black and Jewish leaders in the late 1960s was not a sudden occurrence. The post–World War II literary works of prominent Black writers and the periodic need of Black civil rights leaders to deny, in print, that a tension existed attested to its mounting seriousness. Undoubtedly, however, it was the rise to prominence of a post-King, Black self-determination sentiment that appeared to sound, at the national level, the death knell for what throughout its history had been a fragile but effective relationship between leaders of the two communities. Fueled by the rhetoric of Stokely Carmichael, H. Rap Brown, Eldridge Cleaver, and others who demanded that Black Americans take charge of their own destiny and fanned by disagreements over such strategies for achieving equality as affirmative action, Black and Jewish leaders at the national level entered the decade of the 1970s at considerable odds with one another, with their feud increasingly becoming enmeshed in the larger political battles of the decade and, also increasingly, in the separate agendas of the two communities.

The separate agendas emerged as two wars within the short span of six years served to galvanize the concern of the American Jewish community over the survival of the State of Israel in a manner that exceeded American Jewish support for the ideal of a Jewish homeland over the preceding twenty-five years. The second in this series of Arab-Israeli military conflicts came in 1973, just as Black civil rights leaders were beginning to acknowledge yet another nadir in their long struggle for racial justice in America.

By 1973, it had become clear to most social observers and especially to civil rights leaders that the election of Richard Nixon as the nation's President four years earlier was not a temporary dark cloud over the climate of political liberalism that had characterized the previous decade in American society. Without a prominent national leader to galvanize their efforts, as Martin L. King, Jr. had done until his death, Black civil rights figures were both searching for a new agenda and plausible strategies for rekindling the conscience of the nation, while attempting to sort out the contentious issue of succession to King's leadership.

When they turned to look for allies in the first of these twin tasks, Black leaders encountered a succession of disappointments. Fresh from its second major defeat at the national polls, the Democratic Party—for at least the prior quarter century the political channel for addressing the Black civil rights agenda—had begun its slow retreat from a posture of political liberalism. White liberals, still in disarray over the civil disorders of a decade earlier, dismayed by the campus upheavals of the same period, with their attention diverted by an unpopular war in Southeast Asia and their interests fragmented by a new set of demands—environmental, feminist, and others—for their support, also were sensing the new conservative political climate of the nation and beginning to call for a respite in the vigorous pursuit of civil rights issues and causes. Jewish leadership, preoccupied with Israel and its survival and disenchanted with some elements in the new Black agenda as well as how those elements were being expressed, came to be perceived by Black leadership during this period as abandoning a cause in which they had been among the staunchest of supporters over the preceding six decades.

From the perspective of Black leadership, matters were not helped by the advent during this period of an intellectual movement calling itself neo-liberalism. Some of its principal and most vocal spokespersons were Jewish. Their writings appeared, among other places, in leading Jewish publications,[5] and their critiques of the old liberal agenda, including such issues as affirmative action, which by this time had become tests of faith for Black leadership, were seen as reflections of a lack of genuine commitment to the continuing Black struggle.

In the eyes of the Jewish leadership, there was equal cause for disappointment in the attitudes and actions of Black leaders. Jewish leaders shared, to some degree, in the widespread white liberal dismay over the civil disorders of the previous decade, sensing in them a certain element of anti-semitism where the destruction of Jewish-owned businesses occurred. They were more discomforted by the new Black civil rights agenda. The issue of affirmative action, with its perceived goals and quotas for measuring compliance and progress in employment and university admissions for Black Americans, seemed to reinstate practices that the Jewish community had fought for years to overturn.

Particularly disturbing to Jewish leadership, however, was the new rhetoric of the Black cause. In part, a legacy of the strident calls for self-determination that arose in the 1960s and, to a lesser extent, an outgrowth of the jostling for the leadership mantle that five years after King's murder still had not been conferred; the Black rhetoric of this period made clear that Black leadership would set its own agenda, strategies, and timetable for addressing the problem of race in America. On the fringes of this rhetoric could be heard an occasional expression of anti-Jewish sentiment. For Jewish leaders, this stance was considered to be a display of considerable ingratitude for their past support, a manifestation of political naivete in a nation that had moved discernibly toward a conservative stance on racial issues and, in the case of the anti-Jewish fringe, a renewed expression of the problem of Black anti-semitism.

By the late 1970s, this deepening rift between Black and Jewish leaders had become so polarized that word of a clandstine meeting between Andrew Young, Jr., the first Black United States Ambassador to the United Nations, and representatives of the Palestine Liberation Organization was sufficient to create an uproar in the Jewish community, followed by successful demands for Young's resignation. For Jewish leaders, Young had committed the unpardonable political sin, while, in Black circles, Young had been made an unwitting victim of excessive and misplaced Jewish sensitivity.

Accordingly, the stage was set for a series of further mutual suspicions and misunderstandings, which, by the 1980s, bordered on the vituperative in the leadership camps of both communities. Further inflamed by Black-Jewish physical clashes, primarily in New York City, both sets of leaders began to denounce the other for bad faith or abandonment of their mutual commitments.

## III

It was in such an emotionally poisoned atmosphere that charges of Black anti-semitism began to reemerge. The charges were not new; they had been raised in the past by Jewish leaders and writers and answered with equal candor by their Black counterparts. But the appearance on the national scene in 1984 of the Reverend Jesse Jackson seemed to provide for the Jewish leadership a fresh and relevant occasion for demanding that the charge be taken seriously.

Jackson had been among those in Martin L. King's inner circle and, after King's death, one of the several contenders to succeed him. It was 1984, however, before Jackson achieved sufficient national prominence in his campaign for nomination as the Democratic Party's presidential candidate to preempt the field of Black leaders and to emerge as the principal figure in Black America. From a Jewish perspective, Jackson's rise to prominence was fraught with two major problems.

Earlier in his career, Jackson had journeyed to the Middle East where, among others, he met with Yassir Arafat, leader of the PLO. The American media gave ample coverage to pictures of Jackson embracing Arafat and to Jackson's statements in support of the issue of a homeland for the Palestinian people. In the highly charged atmosphere of the post-1973, Arab-Israeli conflict, Jackson's position was anathema to Jewish leaders; his subsequent embrace of Minister Louis Farrakhan, leader of the Nation of Islam in the United States, only made bad matters worse.

Farrakhan leads a group of Black Muslims whose relatively small numbers are greatly overshadowed by their visibility in Black communities and in the American media. Farrakhan has gained a considerable reputation for his unrelenting anti-semitism in its specific meaning of "Jew-hatred"; he is on record as having made complimentary observations about Adolf Hitler and disparaging comments about the Holocaust. Jackson's initial acceptance of Farrakhan's pledge of political support and, under intense pressure, his seeming lack of haste in rejecting such support reinforced the hostility in the Jewish community toward Jackson and his new leadership position. Subsequently, when Jackson was quoted widely in the media for making several anti-Jewish slurs, his Arafat connection and Farrakhan alliance combined to make him, in the eyes of many Jewish leaders, the new preeminent symbol of Black anti-semitism. In spite of his intensive effort to rid himself of the label and to distance himself from Farrakhan, the American Jewish community continued to view Jackson as such during the course of his highly successful 1988 presidential campaign.

## IV

Currently, the issue of Black anti-semitism—whether it exists and, if so, its nature and extent—continues to be debated actively in Jewish circles and, to a far lesser degree, in Black communities across the nation. In large measure, the debate has moved from the public arena in both communities (with the lingering exception of persistent Jewish misgivings about the Jesse Jackson campaign) and into the journals and monographs of scholars where it continues unabated.

As noted, the debate has been primarily one between leaders of the two communities—executives of major Black and Jewish organizations, writers and intellectual figures, and scholars. It also has been principally a national debate; virtually no attempts have been made to determine the extent to which the perceptions of national Black leaders regarding Jewish people and issues are shared by Black citizens in local communities across the country.

The latter point is of especial importance. Not only have Black and Jewish Americans historically shared a common vision of American society where issues of equality and civil rights are concerned, the patterns of urban growth and development in most major American cities have found Black and Jewish residents living in proximity to one another. In many cities, the waves of internal residential migration have seen upwardly mobile Black families first able to break out of ghetto communities by purchasing homes in predominantly Jewish neighborhoods, a process that has repeated itself as Jewish households have extended their residential areas to the fringes of American cities and into their suburbs. This pattern is still visible in many cities where Black religious and cultural institutions occupy buildings that bear the symbols of their former Jewish occupants.[6]

Some scholars have seen, in this proximity in which Black and Jewish Americans have resided and in their frequent business and commercial contacts, the source of a negative relationship that can be termed "economic anti-semitism" (see Chapter 2, The Literature, following). This relationship warrants continued study and analysis; the concept of economic anti-semitism, however, serves mainly to add further confusion to this task. Economic interactions between two groups may produce prejudice on the part of one group against the other or reciprocal feelings of prejudice on the part of both groups. Whether this relationship and the prejudices it may produce among Black Americans should be elevated to the realm of anti-semitism—in the sense of "Jew-hatred"—is a matter of serious question.

There is, however, a more primary reason for the effort to identify and understand the attitudes of Black Americans—as distinct from those Black leaders—toward the American Jewish populace and to locate such attitudes in the context of contemporary discussions regarding the phenomenon of anti-semitism. It is the reason that provides the major impetus for this study.

One of the widely noted features of Black America is the commitment of its people to religious beliefs and institutions. E. Franklin Frazier, until his death the ranking Black sociologist in the United States, devoted his career primarily to the study of the Black church and the Black family as the two dominant institutions of Black America. "The Negro Church," Frazier has written, "has left its imprint on practically every aspect of Negro life," (1963, p. 85) While Frazier was not enamored with the contemporary role of the Black church, he recognized together with a wide array of scholars the "important role of religion and the Negro church in the social organization of . . . American Negroes" and, by extension, its powerful influence in shaping the attitudes and values of its Black members.

There is also ample evidence that the Black church is an expression of beliefs and values that, while they share much with mainstream Christianity, are different in distinctive ways. In religious institutional affiliation, it is estimated that Black Baptists and Methodists account for four-fifths of the total Black church membership in the United States.[7] Of this number, more than 90 percent belong to historically Black denominations that exist as separate organizations, independent from the ecclesiastical structures of white American Protestantism. American Black Protestantism, there, has a discrete existence institutionally and, to a degree, theologically from that of white Protestant churches.

The history of this distinctive Black Protestantism has produced a Black church that, as scholars have noted, performs a much greater social, educational, and political role in the life of its members than does white Protestantism in America.[8] Both Martin L. King, Jr. and Jesse Jackson, as Black pastors, symbolize at the national level the political role of Black clergy, but their clerical counterparts can be found holding political office or mobilizing their memberships as powerful electoral constituencies in cities and counties all across the nation. Educationally, socially, and culturally, the Black church continues to be an institution around which the nonwork activities of many Black Americans revolve as well as where many of their attitudes, values, and outlooks are shaped.

Finally, scholars note the extent to which Black Protestantism draws upon the Jewish Biblical tradition and experience for its frames of reference in providing a religious interpretation of the Black experience in America. In Black preaching, the themes of slavery and deliverance and of oppression and freedom as experienced by the people of Israel in Biblical times form a distinctive core of the Sunday message. The heroic figures of Biblical Judaism—Moses, David, Saul, and Elijah—are used as models for exhortation and instruction, while the messages of the Hebrew prophets become primary sources for the affirmation of principles regarding social justice and responsibility. In similar fashion, the themes of Black music—particularly Black spirituals and

Gospel music—owe a large debt to these same sources for their inspiration.

## V

The distinctive role and influence of the Black church in the lives of its members, together with the discernible impact of the Jewish biblical tradition on the context and content of Black preaching and other religious interpretations of the Black experience in America, combine to suggest the appropriateness of the query that this study has pursued. Essentially, it is to ask: what are the attitudes of Black American Protestants toward Jewish people in contemporary American society?

Both the query and this study are limited by certain obvious constraints. For one, neither attempts a definitive answer regarding the direct influence of Black Protestant teaching and preaching on the attitudes and values of its adherents, either toward Jewish people or any other issue. Such a relationship may be posited, but it would require a far more extensive inquiry to determine its validity. For another, the study does not purport to be an exhaustive answer to the question it poses. It represents a limited sample of Black Protestant churchgoers in three American cities and, as such, is primarily descriptive rather than nationally significant.

Nonetheless, the findings of this study are sufficiently at variance with much of the current literature and analysis regarding the issue of Black anti-semitism that they suggest the need for considerable caution in the use and application of this term. Those for whom any manifestation of prejudice toward Jewish people is to be equated with anti-semitism may remain unconvinced, but, for others, this small effort to depict what Black Protestants in three American cities think about Jews may serve to enlighten and correct widely held assumptions and perceptions.

# 2
# The Literature

If the volume of literature on the topic is any indication, anti-semitism is a widespread phenomenon among Black Americans. Since World War II, over two thousand books, essays, and monographs have been devoted to the subject, not counting newspaper and magazine articles of a popular or secondary nature. Two extensive bibliographies and six major historical surveys on Black-Jewish relations document the extent to which Black-Jewish encounters have been a matter of significant interest to American writers, scholars, and other intellectuals.

Much of the literature, however, presumes the reality of Black anti-semitism and proceeds to identify and analyze its putative manifestations. Comparatively little effort, noticeable in scholarly circles, had been given to inquiries designed to define the character and features of Black Americans' attitudes toward Jewish people and to determine whether such attitudes fit, within reason, any of the range of possibilities concerning how anti-semitism is to be defined and understood. As a first consequence, therefore, much of the literature is of an impressionistic and anecdotal, rather than empirical, nature.

"Within reason"—as a constraining criterion of definitions of anti-semitism—still manages to embrace a variety of possible attitudes. As a second consequence, one finds numerous examples and references in the literature that purport to describe Black anti-semitism but that must be weighed carefully, in the light of *a priori* judgments regarding what anti-semitism itself is or represents.

# I

While one bibliographic reference traces Black-Jewish relations since 1752 (Davis 1984), the study of attitudes of Black Americans and anti-semitism has its beginnings in the 1930s. During this decade and well into the 1940s, an essentially polite but candid exchange took place between Black and Jewish leaders, writers, and intellectuals; Black commentators appeared in Jewish publications, and articles by Jewish authors were to be found in Black journals (see Shankman 1979; Reddick 1942; Chandler 1942; Richardson 1943 and 1944).

Occasionally, a major literary essay such as Richard Wright's famed autobiography, *Black Boy* (1937), appeared and, for those anxious to establish the existence of Black anti-semitism, became part of the permanent folklore on the topic. With few exceptions, discussions during this period are particularly notable for the lack of sympathy on the part of Black writers with the Nazi, anti-Jewish propaganda that was so prevalent; scholars have cited the Black press (see Wedlock 1942), especially the *New York Age, New York Amsterdam News, Crisis, Messenger, Negro World,* and *Chicago Defender,* for their consistent opposition to anti-semitism and the frequently stated parallel that these publications drew between the Nazi mistreatment of the Jews and that of Black Americans (Davis 1984; Stemons 1941; Bloom 1973). Kenneth Clark (1950) provides a bibliography of the few empirical studies undertaken during this period, noting their methodological immaturity and suggesting the need for better, scientifically valid inquiries on the topic.

Before such work could begin in earnest in the 1950s, three studies of the prior decade laid the groundwork for much of the theory concerning Black-Jewish relations that would come to dominate the subsequent literature. In 1944, Eleanor Wolf et al. published research findings that suggested both Black and Jewish Americans had negative stereotypes of one another, Black Americans perceived Jewish people as such and not as an undifferentiated part of the white populace, and Black resentment of the Jewish populace was related especially to Jewish business activities in Black communities. Three years later, in an article subtitled "A Study of Negro Anti-Semitism", Harold Sheppard (1947) took note of particular anti-Jewish sentiments among Black merchants in Chicago and concluded that "any attempt to explain anti-Semitism among Negroes must go beyond partial—if not superficial— suggestions, such as 'Fascist propaganda' or . . . 'frustration-agression'" and examine, instead, changes in the class structure of Black

American society. Finally, in 1945, two nationally prominent Black sociologists, St. Clair Drake and Horace Cayton, published a landmark study of "Negro life in a northern city" (the book is titled *Black Metropolis* and the city was Chicago) in which they note:

> Because many of the interviews we quote were made when the campaign [ed. note: a small Black newspaper had launched a vitriolic campaign against Jewish merchants] was at its heights, the repeated references to Jews may represent an abnormal situation; in other years, such references might be less frequent. Yet as the most highly visible persons in the community, Jewish merchants tend to become the symbol of the Negro's verbal attack on all white businessmen, and anti-Semitic waves sometimes sweep through Bronzeville [ed. note: Black Chicago]. In New Orleans, where Italian merchants predominate in Negro areas, 'Dagoes' are the target of attack. In Bronzeville it is the Jew who is the scapegoat.

The Drake-Cayton comment is instructive in several respects. For one, it offers a methodological caution regarding the possible influence of dramatic events on responses to attitudinal surveys that too few social scientists would heed in subsequent studies. It also suggests—contra Wolf et al.—that Jewish merchants serve as proximate symbols for white businesses in general. These three studies, however, set the tone for an argument that anti-Jewish sentiments are discernible among Black Americans and, in the instances of Wolf and Sheppard, that such sentiments are specifically directed toward Jews as Jews. These studies also developed two of the six major theories that would emerge in subsequent efforts to explain Black prejudicial attitudes toward Jewish people that already had come to be seen as anti-semitic.

The work of Wolf and Sheppard reinforced, if it did not represent the origins of, an economic theory of Black anti-semitism (i.e., that negative contacts between Black clients and Jewish merchants, landlords and other businesspeople give rise to anti-Jewish attitudes). Drake and Cayton's study would contribute to the "contact theory" of Black anti-semitism (i.e., Jewish individuals are the most immediate and intimate contacts that a significant number of Black Americans have with the white world). The economic theory would be expanded upon by Lenski (1961), Selznick and Steinberg (1969), Gans (1972), and others; it continues as a prominent current interpretation of the source of Black-Jewish tensions.

The "contact theory," which has found equally widespread support among social scientists, has been advanced, among others, by Cothran (1951) who states that:

> southern Negroes are less violently anti-Semitic than northern Negroes . . . because Negroes are forced to live in 'Black ghettos' in many large northern cities. Where Jews are the principal businessmen, they (Negroes) develop latent and overt hostility toward Jews.

Cothran's studies also gave credence to a third explanation or theory of Black attitudes toward Jewish Americans by suggesting that a regional or geographic difference (e.g., between northern and southern Black Americans) could be noted. Earlier work by Bayton and Byoune (1947) and a subsequent study by Prothro and Jensen (1952) added further weight to this geographic explanation, which is echoed, in part, in the more recent work of Quinley and Glock (1979). To these may be added a status theory that Glock et al. (1966) found expressed in a study of American attitudes toward the trial of Adolf Eichmann (and which holds that both Black and white Americans tend more to express anti-semitic attitudes if they have lower educational levels of attainment, income, and prestige status), its reverse in the form of an elite theory (i.e., that it is the "more privileged, knowledgeable" Black American who demonstrates an increasing degree of economic and ideological anti-semitism—in addition to Glock et al., see Tsukashima (1976, 1978, 1979) and, finally, the scapegoat theory suggested by Drake and Cayton but pursued by Berson (1971) and others.

Curiously, many of these early studies, while searching for theories to explain either Black attitudes toward Jews or an anti-semitism already presumed to exist, found Black respondents more positively inclined toward Jewish people than toward other white Americans. Bayton and Byoune found stereotypes of Jewish Americans more positive among Black southerners than elsewhere; Prothro and Jensen discovered "the attitude of the Negro students toward Jews was significantly more favorable than their attitude toward all whites" (although they reasoned that the finding might be caused "more by a low rating of whites than . . . unusual sympathy for Jews"). Cothran similarly remarks on a generally more positive view of Jewish Americans among Black

Americans than the latter's view of non-Jewish, white Americans, and a major national poll conducted in 1963 by Brink and Harris found that Black Americans viewed the Jewish community as helpful—just behind Catholic priests and ahead of white Protestant churches—in the struggle for racial justice.

By the 1950s, however, the idea of Black anti-semitism had found firm lodging in the academic mind and had entered the mainstream of accepted fact, which would be expanded upon and transmitted by subsequent scholarly generations. Summarizing the major negative findings of the period, Simpson and Yinger (1953), whose text, *Racial and Cultural Minorities,* would become a staple of sociology courses in colleges and universities across the nation, asserted that Black Americans (1) share a culture-prevalent anti-semitic attitude, (2) attempt to make their own status appear better by anti-semitic expressions, and (3) include Jews as a distinctive element in a general antiwhite prejudice. Barely a decade after serious scientifically based inquiries on Black attitudes toward Jews had been launched, the academic community had found Black anti-semitism to be widespread and had developed a range of theories to aocount for its occurrence.


## II


As Drake and Cayton would insist that we note, the period 1955–68 was one of rising optimism among Black Americans. Midway through this era that many Black observers came to see as the Second Reconstruction period in American history, a completely unrelated event—the Anti-Defamation League of B'nai B'rith launched the most extensive effort ever undertaken to study anti-semitism in the United States—occurred. Initially contemplated as a five-year inquiry, the study actually spanned the years 1963 to 1975, produced nine volumes of data and interpretations, and resulted in numerous other articles, commentaries, and assessments. The ADL study remains one of, if not *the,* major sources for contemporary viewpoints and perceptions on the topic.

The major work in the ADL series, which addresses directly the issue of Black attitudes toward the Jewish populace, is that of

Gary Marx (1967). This benchmark study examined and summarized the statistical outcomes of previous studies published during the preceding two decades and concluded that "six of seven studies . . . report that Jews are seen (by Black Americans) in a more favorable light than other whites or that less hostility is expressed toward (Jews) than other whites."

Marx sought, in his own analysis, to deal with the frequently posed theories of economic relationships between Black and Jewish Americans and their frequent personal contacts with one another as the source of Black anti-semitism. He found that "only thirteen percent . . . among those with seemingly no predisposition to economically based anti-Semitism . . . scored as anti-Semitic" while "only seventeen percent of those scored as anti-Semitic seem to lack any economic base for their prejudice." He concludes:

> Among Negroes, as among whites, beliefs about Jews are largely determined by contact with the prevailing stereotypes, and the acceptance of these beliefs is no doubt affected by psychological factors. However, for Negroes, anti-Semitic stereotypes appear to be much more related to actual experiences with Jews in the economic world. . . . Where Jews do not predominate in the ghetto, the particular ethnic group that does is likely to be the recipient of economically inspired hostility.

This stated, Marx repeated his overall finding that there was no basis for the accusations of widespread anti-semitism among Black Americans.

"All in all", he writes, ". . . no case can be made for the prevalent notion that anti-Semitism is more widespread among Negroes than among whites, any more than it could be shown that (Negroes) single out Jews for special enmity. . . . Negroes were more likely to accept negative economic stereotypes about Jews than whites. . . . On measures not involving stereotypes, however, Negroes consistently emerge as less anti-Semitic."

Alongside Marx, two other publications appeared in the ADL series that have come to have a much greater impact on the Black anti-semitism debate. The first appeared a year before Marx' study and focused on Christian beliefs and anti-semitism (Glock and Stark, 1966). As a major problem required the authors to discard Black responses from their survey sample, this study does not offer any useable data concerning the question of Black anti-semitism. The second volume, published the same year (Glock et al.) focues on Black and white attitudes expressed toward the trial of Adolf Eichmann. This study found that both Black and white Americans tend to express greater anti-semitic attitudes the lower their scores related to status, educational level, income, and other social prestige factors.

In the Eichmann study, the authors acknowledge that their sample of Black respondents was too small to permit statistically valid findings. In spite of this major limitation, the study offers two intriguing observations:

> As to the role of anti-Semitism, it apparently did not occur to the Negro any more than it did to the white that this was a matter to be considered in forming his judgments (regarding the trial). There is no evident anti-Semitic effect. Again, it is not clear whether this is a result of the lack of salience of the trial to the Negro or the lack of salience of anti-Semitism itself.

In their analysis of the responses in this study, Glock et al. found similarity between Black and white attitudes on most of the survey details, such as "was the trial a good thing?" "Was the judgment correct?" "Does it give you greater sympathy for Jews?" ". . . for Israel?" On these questions, Black and white respondents scored within a few points of each other. A major divergence in the Black and white responses occurred, however, when they were analyzed according to a "legal sophistication" factor: in contrast to white respondents, the more sophisticated Black respondents ranked in legal terms, the less critical they were of the trial while less sophisticated Black respondents were more critical, leading the authors to note that "in this respect, the relationship between being sophisticated and being critical was exactly the opposite in the Negro community from what it was in the white community."

This somewhat startling finding caused the authors to conclude:

> Whites and Negroes of comparable status and knowledge followed quite different courses in deciding their answers to the questions on over-all effect, and the similarity in the results is a statistical artifact. . . . This discussion . . . has served the important function . . . of suggesting that, even when they share similar or apparently similar

economic statuses in society, the Negro views events from a perspective different from that of the white.

## III

The assassination of Martin Luther King, Jr. in the spring of 1968 and the election, in November of that year, of Richard Nixon as president of the United States brought the civil rights era, with its rising Black expectations and significant Black progress on many fronts, to an end. The years that followed are marked by a discernible shift in the character, tenor, and findings of research on the issue of Black anti-semitism.

On a positive note, the year 1969 opened with a publication by Peter Goldman that reported the outcomes of his analysis of *Newsweek* magazine polling data from the years 1963, 1966, and 1969. Goldman concluded that the extent of Black anti-semitism had been greatly exaggerated during this period, in part due to the rhetoric of "Black militants" and a corresponding tendency of the media to overplay their comments. "The result," he wrote, "was a good deal of hysteria in the Jewish establishment," followed by a breakdown in the alliance between Black and Jewish civil rights leaders.

Based on the *Newsweek* data, Goldman concluded:

> . . . the Jews were substantially more popular with Negroes than white people generally were. . . . Negroes differentiate between Whites and Jews . . . what [Black] animosity there was against [Jews] existed less because they are Jewish than because they are white.

The same year another in the ADL series appeared under the title, *The Tenacity of Prejudice: Anti-Semitism in Contemporary America*. The study was presented as "a representative cross section of the national population" (in 1964) although its authors (Selznick and Steinberg, 1969), as in several of the previous studies examined, acknowledge ". . . the small size of [its] Negro sample." In spite of this significant constraint, the authors advance several major observations regarding Black anti-semitism and come to several significant conclusions:

It should come as no surprise that anti-Semitism exists among Negroes. It would be illusory to think that, because they are an oppressed minority, Negroes reject anti-Semitic stereotypes which, to some degree, characterize every segment of American society. The issue is not whether anti-Semitism is prevalent among Negroes, but the extent to which it exists.

Selznick and Steinberg proceed to explore these primary questions: (1) "Are Negroes, in fact, more anti-Semitic than whites, as is often implied? (2) Does anti-Semitism among Negroes differ in content or kind from that found among whites? (3) Is the quality of Negro-Jewish contacts a factor in Negro anti-Semitism? As findings to these questions, they report that:

(1) In the economic area, Negroes are more anti-Semitic than whites. In the non-economic area, no consistent differences exist. (2) Among Negroes, as whites, greater education is associated with lower rates of anti-Semitism. Nevertheless, Negroes continue to be higher in economic anti-Semitism even when compared to whites at the same educational level. (3) One of the more striking findings . . . and one that is consistent with the view that Negro anti-Semitism is rising—is that acceptance of anti-Semitic beliefs is disproportionately high in the youngest as well as the oldest age group. . . . Though young Negroes are more educated than older Negroes, they are no less anti-Semitic.

The "more striking finding" of Selznick and Steinberg identified a significant problem that subsequent research would explore in greater depth. However, it is their initial observation that "the issue is not whether anti-Semitism is present among Negroes but the extent to which it exists" that would become the operating premise of most subsequent inquiries on the topic.

As tensions mounted and mutually recriminatory opinions were uttered by both Black and Jewish Americans in the late 1960s and throughout the 1970s, the studies of Black anti-semitism continued unabated. At one level, polling data about Black-Jewish relations suggested little change, if any, in the generally favorable attitudes of Black toward Jewish Americans (see Harris and Swanson 1970). At another, researchers continued to find specific loci of anti-semitism among Black Americans: urban "Black militants" (Shuman and Hatchett 1974), those with more frequent economic contacts and relationships (Forster and Epstein 1974; Martire and Clark 1982), and Black Nationalists (Forster and Epstein). Studies such as that of Weisbord and Stein (1970) continued to conclude that ". . . classical anti-Semitism has never curdled the emotions nor perverted the behavior of Black people," while other works (e.g., Halpern 1971) insisted on recognizing the ideological sentiments of "Black militants" as a new source of anti-semitism among Black Americans.

During this period, while academic studies essentially attached themselves to either a defense or a denial of the Black anti-semitism proposition, a spate of popular articles on the topic were appearing that tended to state the argument—generally in support of the idea—in much less cautious or documented terms. These works, in large measure, were responses to specific occurrences in the 1960s, including a bitter struggle and resultant teachers' strike in New York City over the issue of community control of schools (the Ocean Hill–Brownsville controversy), the civil disorders in mid-decade that gave rise to disputes over the presence or absence of Black hostility toward Jewish businesses in the burning of the urban Black ghettoes, and the reactions to comments made by Black participants at several national consultations convened to discuss and, hopefully, to ameliorate the rising tide of Black-Jewish tensions (see, for example, Lester 1979; Friedman 1979; Belth 1979; Teller 1970; Wilkins 1977).

Without question, public expressions of a small circle of Black writers in the 1960s lent credence to the increasing charges of Black anti-semitism. Le Roi Jones (Amiri Baraka) in Newark, whose poetry contributed to the concept of Negritude and who laments the "patronizing condescension" of Jewish and other white liberals toward Black Americans (Jones and Neal 1966; Jones 1972) and Ron Karenga in Los Angeles (Halisi and Mtume 1967) are representative of this new Black thought. At a more sophisticated level, Harold Cruse (1967) presented an extended critique of the Black-Jewish alliance, arguing that Black Americans had yielded intellectual leadership to Jews and thereby forfeited the leadership of their own struggle.

These commentaries evoked the recollection of an earlier period in which other Black writers and intellectuals had spoken, with more charity but with equal candor, about their misgivings regarding Black-Jewish relations. Kenneth Clark's commentary (1946) and James Baldwin's early writings (1948, 1955) were raised as examples of a virtually unbroken thread of Black hostility toward Jewish Americans. Both local and national meetings of Black and Jewish spokespersons, called to find ways of reducing these tensions, seemed only to heighten them. The venerable Black educator, Horace Mann Bond, at one such meeting spoke of a childhood incident in Atlanta in which he and a Jewish playmate exchanged racially charged epithets with each other. Bond's comments, like the earlier personal accounts of Baldwin, would enter the literature for the next two decades as an example of anti-semitism (see Whitfield 1987). The meetings themselves are described as occurring in rooms that "seemed to sweat with hate" and as scenes in which Black and Jewish participants were at one another's throats (see Feuerlicht 1983; Bontemps 1974).

Almost as if the rhetorical debate between leaders of the two communities had grown too shrill and the social science studies too inconclusive, a wealth of historical volumes began to be published during this period, which by their appearance suggested that the issue of Black anti-semitism needed to be placed in context and perspective. A study of the Jewish community in the South (Dinnerstein 1973), of Jewish-Black relations at the turn of the twentieth century (Foner 1975), of Jewish and Black leaders in the period 1915–35 (Diner 1977) together with works by Shankman (1975), Hertzberg (1978), Hellwig (1973), Labovitz (1975), and others sought to display the enormous range of events and circumstances that had brought Black and Jewish Americans into contact with one another since the American colonial era. These studies served to document and illustrate the contours of a relationship that, like all intimate encounters, had never been consistently smooth or benign but, in the main, positive. While these studies contributed immensely to an enlargement of understanding on the issue, they did little, unfortunately, to moderate the ferocity of the debate.

# IV

In the prolonged and, at times, painful history of the debate on Black anti-semitism, at least two features are apparent. First, a significant amount of theory, findings, and conclusions have been developed with little documented evidence to support them. Clark in 1950 lamented the lack of scientific studies on the issue, and Howard Fast (1967) echoed Clark's observation by noting seventeen years later that "no one has ever done a scientific or even pseudo-scientific study of the state of anti-Semitism among the Negro people." Nevertheless, studies on the topic continued to abound, an inordinate number of which acknowledge the inadequacy of their Black sample populace or the absence of statistically useable data on the basis of which valid conclusions could be drawn. The relatively few major inquiries that have addressed the question directly and that in large measure have found no empirical support for the thesis have been largely ignored. Second, surprisingly little empirical attention has been given to the religious factor and its possible impact on Black attitudes toward Jewish people. It is particularly surprising in light of the attention given this factor in analyses of anti-semitism as a general phenomenon.

Charles Glock, whose major contribution to the study of anti-semitism in America has been noted earlier, also produced (with Rodney Stark) in the same year in which he presented the volume on attitudes toward the Eichmann trial, a major study on Christian beliefs and anti-semitism (1966) as part of the ADL series. It remains a seminal work on this topic and offers a strong case for the linkage between conservative Protestant beliefs and anti-semitism. Glock and Stark argue that orthodox religious beliefs lead Christians to take an exclusionist view of their and other religious faiths, which, among other things, holds "the historic Jew" responsible for the crucifixion of Jesus and results in an extension of this hostility toward all Jewish people. (The theological analysis of this position has been presented forcefully by a group of Christian theologians critical of conventional Christian teaching regarding relationships between Jews and Christians (see Littell 1975).

For methodological reasons, Glock and Stark were unable to test their hypothesis on a sample of Black Protestants. Nevertheless, their thesis produced a chorus of rejoinders that took issue with their methodology and their conclusions (see Middleton

1973; Roof 1975). None of this debate addresses the issue of Black Protestant beliefs, although the thesis itself is of major importance to such an issue.

A year earlier, Marx, in the ADL series, also had posed a set of hypotheses regarding the religious factor in Black attitudes toward Jewish people. Working from his general conclusion that Black Americans "see Jews in a more favorable light than they see non-Jewish whites," Marx suggests:

> As Christians, Negroes may have developed or absorbed hostile beliefs about Jews as religious outsiders. However, unique to the Negro, and a factor possibly working to produce positive feelings for Jews, was Negro slavery and identification with the Israelites of the Old Testament . . . as another people of bondage who struggled and obtained their freedom.

Nevertheless, by 1966, books and articles began to appear that cite classical Christian teachings about Jews, Christian fundamentalism, general assumptions about "the tradition of anti-Semitism in the Christian world," and even comments of Black writers on Black religion, all as putative sources of Black anti-semitism. Significantly, none of these works offer any supporting evidence for their assertions.

What these commentaries lack in evidence, however, they more than make up for in conviction. Duker (1969), for example, writes:

> We should take it for granted that anti-semitism among Negroes basically stems from the same sources which have nurtured Jew-hatred among white Christians, namely, theological Deicide notions. . . . Negro Christians have been raised on the same new Testament perhaps more so than white Christians. It is likely that many have absorbed anti-Jewish theological teachings and folklore.

Judd Teller, in 1966, claims:

> The Jewish community had apparently assumed that of all Christian generations the contemporary Negro somehow would be immune from a condition that is indigenous to universal Christianity, has always provided release for the underprivileged of Christian society and has sometimes been used by its leaders to deflect the rabble's wrath from themselves. . . . Christian fundamentalism, which the Negro and whites share, is the first and primary source of Negro anti-

Semitism. . . . anti-Semitism remains the insoluble bond between the Klan and Negro anti-Semitism.

And the Sobels (1969) declare:

Given the overwhelming predominance of Protestant fundamentalism within the Negro community, as well as the ambiguous role of the Jew in this tradition, it need not be surprising that a religious basis for Jew-hatred can be said to exist here.

Once again, on an issue left undecided by the social scientists and enflamed by popular commentaries, the historians took up the challenge of providing a perspective on the question. Shankman (1979) notes the Black church as a major source of knowledge about Jewish people, both Biblical and contemporary, and cites essentially positive expressions of Black preachers toward Jews in both periods. Hertzberg (1978) cites the emulation themes expressed in Black literature—the notions that Israelite bondage, deliverance, suffering, and freedom had produced laudable traits among the modern Jewish populace, such as family solidarity, hard work, and high esteem for education that Black Americans would do well to follow. Evans (1973), Foner (1975), and others offered historical analyses that generally support the conclusion of Rose (1983):

While it has been argued that 'if Blacks are anti-Semitic, it is because they are Christian', most evidence belies such a claim. One must look elsewhere for roots of whatever Black anti-Semitism exists.

One of the most recent studies on anti-semitism (Martire and Clark 1982) essentially brings the discussion up to date. Based on the earlier work of Selznick and Steinberg, it was designed to measure the trends in anti-semitism over the preceding two decades. As a summary of their findings, the authors state:

Prejudice against Jews is most likely to be found among non-Jews who are less educated, older (55 and older or retired), living in cities, or black.

With respect to the religious factor, these authors write:

The current study indicates . . . that the relationship between Christian orthodoxy and anti-Semitism is due almost entirely to three demographic factors: education, race, and age. . . . (Although there is a slight but significant positive statistical relationship between religious conservatism and anti-Semitism) after controlling for education, race, and age, we find that the partial correlation between religiousness and anti-Semitism virtually disappears, indicating that the apparent relationship is actually due to the fact that individuals who are traditional in their religious outlook are more likely to be older, less educated and [*sic*] Black—all factors that are associated with higher levels of anti-Semitic belief.

Finally, with specific reference to Black Americans, Martire and Clark note, as past studies have indicated, that northern, urban Black residents are more anti-semitic than non-Black northern urbanites, that more education and age do not mitigate Black anti-semitic attitudes, that Black anti-semitism has little to do with Jewish ethnicity or religion but, instead, is typically expressed in the language of economic criticisms. They conclude:

Blacks are as likely or more likely to accept Jews as they are Italian Americans as neighbors, political candidates, or marriage partners for their children. The one issue that appears to separate Jews from other ethnic groups in the view of Blacks is the perceived business power of Jews: 40% believe Jews have too much power in the business world, compared to 28% who feel that way about Italian Americans and 17% who feel that way about Japanese Americans. . . . To the extent that black prejudice against Jews is uniquely directed against Jews, it appears to stem from economic sources.

Thus, on the eve of the study on which this volume reports, the economic theory of Black anti-semitism continues to hold sway. Clearly, however, it has not muted the claim that Christian beliefs also lie at the core of Black prejudice toward Jewish people. The study that follows offers a modest but one of the few empirical attempts undertaken to address this latter question.

# 3

# A Survey of Black Protestant Attitudes Toward Jewish Americans in Three U.S. Cities: The Douglas Institute Survey

## RAYMOND G. HUNT

In 1986, the Anti-Defamation League commissioned the consulting firm of Tarrance, Hill, Newport, and Ryan to undertake a follow-on and extension of Glock and Stark's survey of two decades earlier regarding Christian beliefs and anti-semitism. The Tarrance study was a national telephone survey of one thousand evangelical Protestant Christians, defined as members of "either conservative or moderate American denominations, who reported that religion was of major importance to them in their daily lives, and who reported frequent church attendance." In addition to Episcopalians, Presbyterians, Congregationalists, and Unitarians, the Tarrance survey also excluded Black respondents.

The William O. Douglas Institute's 1986 survey on which this volume reports, while less rigorous than the Tarrance work, focuses expressly on Black Protestants, similarly defined and questioned. It therefore supplements the Tarrance survey and provides opportunities for racial comparisons.

## Sample

Convenience samples of volunteers from several predominantly Black churches in three different cities (Seattle, St. Louis, and Buffalo) responded to a multi-item, self-administered questionnaire. A total of 189 usable questionnaires resulted (37 from Buffalo, 36 from St. Louis, and 116 from Seattle).

Two-thirds of the respondents were female (as opposed to 52% in the Tarrance study) in the total sample. The age range of the sample is given in Table 1, from which can be seen its concentration of middle-aged persons (31–50 years old). The present sample, then, was somewhat younger overall that the Tarrance survey, especially in the youngest groups (6% under 25 in the Tarrance research; about 18% in this study). It was also a comparatively well-educated group (65% having at least some college, unlike the 45% in the Tarrance survey), that nevertheless was concentrated (53%) in income levels under $20,000 (see Tables 2 and 3). The Tarrance sample had a smaller percentage of low-income respondents (33% under $20,000) and a higher percentage (17% as compared with 9%) in the over $40,000 bracket. Nearly 50% of the respondents were Baptists (see Table 4, where the "other" category includes principally twenty-four individuals who were United Methodist, a number that in fact makes them the second most-represented denomination in the sample). Thus, Baptists and Methodists were predominant in this sample as they were, albeit less so, in the Tarrance sample. Considering the racial composition of the two samples, they are clearly similar as to denominational affiliation.

On average, respondents from Seattle were somewhat older and better educated than those from Buffalo and St. Louis and had higher incomes. Respondents from Buffalo had lower incomes than those from St. Louis. In the aggregate, the sample covered a broad range of population characteristics, but because of the heavier proportionate representation of the Seattle group, it may be somewhat biased toward influences associated with higher age, education, and income.

Nevertheless, there were few questions the answers to which varied significantly across the three cities and none at all on the key questions defining their religious postures. These questions included items and scales to measure the character, intensity, and particularity of respondents' religious beliefs and practices. These can be summarized as follows for the sample as a whole.

*Religious:*

(a) *Conviction:* (two items [nos. 8 and 9 in the questionnaire to be found in the Appendix to this chapter]). To an item asking about belief in the existence of God, 96% answered either that they had no doubts (88%) or that they may have some doubt but definitely believed (8%). To an item asking about the status of Jesus, 94% responded either that he was the Divine Son of God and they had no doubts about it (91%) or they believed in his divinity despite some doubts (3%).

(b) *Biblical Literalism:* to an item (no. 10) asking about miracles reported in the Bible, 76% said they believed the miracles actually happened just as described, and another 13% said they believed at least some of them did.

These three items (nos. 8, 9, 10) were taken from Glock and Stark (1965). They correspond to what Glock and Stark defined as an "Orthodoxy Index." According to Glock and Stark's scoring system, our respondents earned an index of 2.5, on the average, of a possible 3.0.

(c) *Religious Particularism:* (three items, also from Glock and Stark [nos. 11, 12, and 13]) Particularism refers to the belief in one's own religious beliefs as correct and essential to finding favor with God. Of the respondents 86% said they believed faith in Jesus Christ as Savior was "absolutely essential for salvation." While 43% said that being a member of their particular faith was "absolutely essential for salvation" (another 20% said it would help, but 23% said it "probably would have no influence"); 30% said being ignorant of Jesus Christ would "definitely prevent salvation," 25% said it "possibly would," while 35% said it probably would have no influence.

The average of responses to these three items yielded a Glock and Stark Particularism Index of 3.8 (of a possible 6.0).

(d) *Religious Practice* (Importance in Daily Life): Of the respondents 60% reported attending Sunday worship services (item 14) every week, and another 20% reported going "two or three times a month;" 78% reported saying grace before all meals or at least once a day (item 15).

Items 14 and 15 are also Glock and Stark items that correspond to their Ritualism Dimension. Using the Glock and Stark classification scheme, 55% of our respondents were "high" on this dimension, 21 were "medium," and the rest "low."

(e) *Devotionalism* (items 16 and 17): these items are also from Glock and Stark. Of our sample, 25% said they privately prayed regularly at least once a day (10% said they did so several times a week, and 18% said they prayed often but not at regular intervals. Finally, 85% of the respondents said that prayer was "extremely important" in their lives. Using Glock and Stark's coding, 36% of our sample was classified "high" and 49% "medium" on this dimension.

(f) *Religious Evangelism* was measured by a series of twelve items (items 18a through e on the questionnaire) developed by Putney and Middleton (1961) that tapped both depth of religious conviction, particularism, belief in sin, the Devil and Hell, and belief in helping "those who are confused about religion." The mean rating (on six-point scales) of these twelve items was 4.8, indicative of moderately strong "evangelicalism."

Items 18a–f Putney and Middleton called an "Orthodoxy Scale." Its maximum value is 36. Our sample had an average score of 31.1. Meanwhile, items g–l define a "Fanaticism Scale" with a maximum value of 30. Our respondents had an average score of 27.6.

(g) *Religiosity:* a series of six items, also from Putney and Middleton, measured the "centrality" of religion as an organizing focus for a person's worldview and self-perception (item 19a–f). The mean response to these questions (using six-point scales) was 5.4, indicating high religiosity—i.e., that religion is central to the respondents' approach to life. The maximum value on what Putney and Middleton called an "Importance Scale" is 36. Our respondents earned an average score on six items of 31.7.

*Recapitulation:*

The present sample of Black Protestants is one for whom religion is very important in their daily lives and world views. It may be characterized as having (1) firm convictions about Christian basics; (2) a generally literalistic interpretation of Biblical content; (3) a clearly but tolerantly particularistic view of the correctness and necessity to salvation of their personal religious beliefs; and (4) a moderately evangelical orientation that accompanies their high religiosity. In all these respects it is very similar to the religious characteristics of the Tarrance study's white sample, although somewhat less particularistic.

*Racial Prejudice:*

In addition to the questionnaire items on religious belief just described, the Douglas Institute survey included a ten-item series measuring attitudes about race prejudice generally and whites in particular (item 20a–j). These items were developed during the Douglas Institute's studies of institutional racism in police departments (see Hunt and McCadden 1980). The mean rating (on a six-point scale) of the item, "Race prejudice is universal. It has always been with us, and it always will be," was 4.7. This suggests a somewhat pessimistic general view on the inevitability of prejudice.

The remaining nine items dealt more particularly with attitudes toward whites—their character, bigotry, trustworthiness, and so on. The mean rating on these nine items was 2.5, indicating a generally neutral to charitable attitude toward whites.

Thus, the present sample of Black Protestants is not notably biased against whites, although it tends to regard racial prejudice as endemic to the human condition.

*Anti-semitic/Anti-Jewish Attitudes:*

In the sample of Black respondents for this survey, 56% reported having personal contacts with Jews either "occasionally" or "very often." They describe these contacts mostly as involving coworkers, friends, storekeepers, other businesspeople, or professionals.

(a) *Religiously Based Anti-semitism:* A question raised in the Tarrance study was whether "evangelical Christians hold anti-Semitic views which are based directly on the Christian's religious views." The Douglas Institute survey included three items that broached this issue (21a,f,i). Along with their mean ratings (on six-point scales), the items were as follows:

(1) "The Jews must be considered a bad influence on Christian culture and civilization." (2.3—slight to moderate disagreement).

(2) "Jews may have moral standards which they apply in their dealings with others, but with Christians they are unscrupulous, ruthless, and undependable." (2.5—slight to moderate disagreement).

(3) "The true Christian can never forgive the Jews for their crucifixion of Christ." (1.8—moderate to strong disagreement).

Similar to the findings in the Tarrance survey, the responses to these questions, and especially the third, give no indication of even weak religiously based, collective anti-semitism in this sample of Black Protestants. Furthermore, if anything, the suggestions of religiously based anti-semitism here are *weaker still* than those reported in the Tarrance survey for whites.

(b) *Secular Anti-semitism:* In the Tarrance research, this was defined as negative beliefs about Jews that were not based directly or explicitly on religion. The Douglas Institute survey included a set of items bearing on secular anti-semitism. One subset of these items dealt with attitudes toward *Jews as individuals or as a group* (items 21b,d,g,j,m,q). The overall mean response to these six items (on a six-point scale) was 2.7, indicative of mild disagreement with questions such as the following:

"A major fault of the Jews is their conceit, overbearing pride, and their idea that they are the chosen race." (2.3)

"One trouble with Jewish businessmen is that they stick together and connive, so that a Gentile doesn't have a fair chance in competition with them." (3.1)

"I believe that Jews have too much power in the business world." (2.7)

"On the whole Jews have probably contributed less to American life than any other group." (2.5)

"Jews should stop complaining about the Holocaust." (2.6)

Another subset of items (k,n,o,r) had to do with attitudes toward *Israel.* The mean rating for these four items was 3.6, indicating some anti-Israeli sentiments. These were the mean ratings of individual items:

"Even though Jews always complain about their persecution . . . the Israelis today are guilty of treating the Palestinians in the same manner." (3.8)

"Jews are more loyal to Israel than to America." (3.7—somewhat agree)

"Peace will never come to the Middle East, not because of the Arabs but because of the inflexibility and arrogance of the Israelis." (3.1—slightly agree)

"The Arabs . . . will never rest until they have driven the Jews from Palestine. . . . the Israelis have every right to . . . protect their land." (3.2—slightly agree)

Plainly, the respondents hold more negative attitudes to Israel than to Jews, per se, along with some sympathy with the Palestinian Arabs. These sentiments, which arguably are *not* anti-semitic, are a significant component of overall sentiments toward Jews in this sample. For instance, the overall mean rating of the nineteen secular anti-semitic items was 2.9, which is mildly favorable (i.e., not anti-semitic). This figure becomes a still more favorable 2.7 when the Israel-related items are excluded.

The survey also included five "*pro-Jewish*" items (c,e,h,l,s). The mean rating of these items was 3.4, suggesting a mildly pro-Jewish orientation. The specific items with their ratings are as follows:

"I think of Jews as being almost Black. They know how it feels to be mistreated." (3.8)

"Deep down inside Jews are not as prejudiced as other whites." (3.4)

"Jews are more willing to combat discrimination." (3.6)

"Jews are more helpful than harmful in the civil rights struggle." (3.8)

"Blacks prefer doing business with Jews to non-Jews." (2.5)

Thus, on each of these items the respondents tend to agree with the pro-Jewish statement, except in the case of preferring to do business with Jews, with which they tended to disagree. Most likely this reflects less a prejudice against doing business with Jews than it does indifferences.

Finally, a single item (21p) measured "sympathy" for Jews in dealing with "Black militants." The mean rating to the statement following was 2.6, suggesting some disagreement:

"Unless Jewish leaders and groups put the anti-Jewish black militants in their place, there will be a lot more anti-Semitism."

Respondents were asked to rank five Black leaders for the "esteem" (or respect) in which they were held. Table 5 describes the frequency of ranks for each leader. (In the table, "1"is the highest and "5" the lowest rank; "8" represents the response "don't know"). It can be seen from Table 5 that Andrew Young was both the best known and the most respected of the five leaders. The next best known but least respected was the anti-semite Louis Farrakhan. (Jesse Jackson's ratings here reflect perceptions in 1986.)

Four specimen cases (item 24A–D) were presented to respondents. In each of them, a Jewish person was the object of discrimination on the basis of being Jewish. In each case, the respondents disapproved of the action, most strongly in the case of intermarriage and least strongly in the case of admission to medical school. The ratings on a six-point scale for each case were as follows:

CASE A: 2.4

CASE B: 5.3 (approval of *rejection* of an anti-Jewish action)

CASE C: 1.7

CASE D: 1.7

## Discussion and Conclusion

The essential conclusion of the Tarrance survey was that a majority of white Protestants showed no anti-semitism; and there were some indications that evangelical Christians were, on the whole, more positive to Jews than were Christians generally. From the findings reported here, the same can be said of Black Protestants. If anything they appear to be less anti-Jewish than their white counterparts. Certainly there are no indications here of significant anti-semitic sentiments, although some skepticism exists about Israel and its treatment of the Palestinian Arabs.

Therefore, to the essential query posed for this study, namely, "what are the attitudes of Black Protestants toward Jewish people in contemporary American society?" we can answer: generally tolerant and largely favorable. They are plainly not anti-semitic and, on the whole, quite like the white Protestants surveyed in the Tarrance project.

Table 1
Percentage Age Distribution

| | |
|---|---|
| < 25 | 18 |
| 26–40 | 32 |
| 41–60 | 38 |
| > 60 | 10 |
| unknown | 2 |

Table 2
Educational Levels (in percent)

| < 12 Years | 12 |
| 12 Years | 20 |
| 13–14 | 26 |
| > 15 Years | 40 |
| Unknown | 2 |

Table 3
Income Levels (in percent)

| < $20,000 | 53 |
| 21–40,000 | 31 |
| > 40,000 | 10 |
| Unknown | 6 |

Table 4
Protestant Denomination (in percent)

| Methodist (AME, ZION, CME) | 14 |
| Baptist | 48 |
| Pentecostal/Holiness | 12 |
| Other *(see text) | 15 |
| Unknown | 11 |

Table 5
Esteem for Selected Black Leaders (in percent)

*Esteem Rating* (1—highest)

| Leader | 1 | 2 | 3 | 4 | 5 | 8* |
|---|---|---|---|---|---|---|
| Andrew Young | 36 | 22 | 08 | 05 | 01 | 28 |
| Walter Fauntleroy | 02 | 08 | 13 | 19 | 09 | 49 |
| Jesse Jackson | 27 | 13 | 07 | 02 | 03 | 48 |
| Louis Farrakhan | 05 | 03 | 08 | 09 | 29 | 46 |
| Benjamin Hooks | 04 | 12 | 14 | 05 | 05 | 60 |

*8—don't know

# References

Glock, C. and Stark, R. 1965. *Christian Beliefs and Anti-Semitism.* New York: Harper & Row.

Putney, S. and Middleton, R. 1961. Dimensions and correlates of religious ideologies. *Social Forces* 39: 285–290.

Tarrance, Hill, Newport, and Ryan. 1966. National Attitudes Survey: September. Unpublished Report.

Hunt, R. G. and McCadden, K. S. 1980. Race-related attitudes and beliefs of police personnel. *Social Development Issues* 4: 31–48.

# 4

# Black Protestantism and Anti-Semitism: A Reappraisal

It is difficult to review more than a half century of study, discussion, and debate on the issue of Black anti-semitism without reaching the conclusion that either we have not learned a great deal or that what we know, based on careful historical studies and social science research, has had little impact on perceptions regarding this topic. With few exceptions, the studies and research data confirm what essayists and popular commentators observed and people on the street reported when the question of Black attitudes toward Jewish people first began to command attention.

Generally, the historians and social scientists have found that Black Americans, over most of this century, have developed views of Jewish Americans based on two distinctly different sets of relationships. One is personal and economic in nature and arises out of contacts in which Black people have been customers of Jewish merchants, tenants of Jewish landlords, domestics in Jewish households, or employees of Jewish businesspeople. This relationship has produced both positive and negative stereotypes of Jews: their devotion to family, work, and education or their capacity for "sticking together" and "helping their own kind" is seen as something to be admired and emulated, while their "shrewdness" in business dealings or their willingness to exploit customers and workers are considered as circumstances against which one should be on guard.

The other relationship is communal and spiritual. It involves, on the part of Black people who have deep religious attachments and convictions, an identification with the Jewish religious tradition—a sense that both peoples have known slavery and oppression and that surely as one has found deliverance and freedom,

59

so will the other. This second relationship is more abstract and less immediate; it is all the more remarkable that it persists, well over a century after Black emancipation and in an era in American society in which religious sentiments must compete with other powerful claims on the consciences and convictions of Black citizens.

Obviously, these two different viewpoints are not compatible. They undoubtedly operate so as to effect what several scholars have termed a "bittersweet encounter" between Black and Jewish Americans. To complicate matters, they are viewpoints that can exist side by side; they may be held simultaneously by Black individuals who, in one moment or circumstance, will speak disparagingly of an experience with "a Jew" and, in another, describe with equal conviction his or her admiration for Jewish family and educational values, express appreciation for Jewish support of the Black struggle for racial justice and equality, and proclaim devotion to a God who is perceived to have given Jewish and Black people alike a common historical experience.

The question of what is to be made of all this remains elusive. Is it possible to hold both positive and negative stereotypes, or is the one the "real" view and the other only a romanticized abstraction? Have the mounting disagreements over civil rights goals and strategies stained the positive images that Black Americans have held toward Jewish people and reinforced their negative perceptions? Is the quarrel of Black America today with the American Jewish community that the latter has become more American than Jewish? And if all the negative stereotypes, sentiments, and perceptions are added up, do they equate to what may be called properly: Black anti-semitism? How are we to sort out, make sense of, and especially, weigh these varying and ambivalent reactions that appear to characterize the Black perspective on Black-Jewish relations in America?

To the casual observer, stereotypes might seem to be the easiest in a list of admittedly difficult questions. They are vices to which nearly everyone is subject and, for most, minor ones at best. Lawyers find themselves on the receiving end of numerous sterotypes these days—none of them positive. Scholars tend to think of themselves and their peers as a special breed of humanity, somehow set apart from, if not superior to, the rest of the common crowd.

Many people have unfavorable impressions of motorcyclists—particularly those who travel in packs, two abreast, down two-lane thoroughfares; martini drinkers are apt to view beer lovers as unsophisticated; devotees of Bach are not likely to hold fans of hard rock in high esteem. We are apt to consider these foibles as relatively innocent and reasonably benign, as long as we do not act upon them in discriminatory or aggressive ways.

When our stereotypes are positive, we are even less inclined to view them as problematic. Physicians and surgeons, in spite of the burgeoning increase in malpractice suits, continue to enjoy a certain mystique in modern society; most people defer to their judgments, follow their advice, and treat them with an uncommon respect. The hard-driving corporate executive who heads a gigantic business enterprise has become something of a folk hero in modern times, particularly during the past eight years when political and popular rhetoric have reinforced the notion that activities of the private sector are the source of everything that is good, virtuous, and wholesome in America. And in spite of the scandals that have toppled several nationally prominent televangelists from their perches, opinion polls show that many people have a positive image of the clergy and those in religious orders.

In the context of discussions of anti-semitism, however, stereotypes illustrate the complexity of the issue and, with particular regard to Black anti-semitism, the sharpness of the debate that continues to surround it. A recent scholarly exchange in a noted historical journal provides a pertinent case-in-point.

The November 1986 issue of the *American Jewish Archives* contains an article by Leonard Dinnerstein (whose edited volume on *Jews in the South* has been cited earlier) on "The Origins of Black Anti-Semitism in America." Dinnerstein argues that Black antipathy toward Jewish people has been "built upon a layer of enunciated prejudices" drawn from Protestantism and the folklore of white European culture, which have served to produce the stereotypes, in the first instance, of Jews as Christ-killers and, in the second, of the "cunning and exploitative Jew whose ruthlessly amassed fortune is used to acquire political and economic control of society. . . ." Dinnerstein finds the general acceptance of these stereotypes in much of the Black press of the 1920s and 1930s, which, together with excerpts from the writings and public comments of such eminent Black figures as Booker T. Washington, W. E. B. DuBois, James Weldon Johnson, Richard Wright, and James Baldwin, he offers as evidence of Black anti-semitism.

Dinnerstein's article provoked a sharp rebuttal from Stephen Whitfield, which appeared a year later in the same journal ("A Critique of Leonard Dinnerstein's 'The Origins of Black Anti-Semitism in America'"). Whitfield asserts:

> Though the evidence itself is incontrovertible (and could no doubt be enlarged), its meaning has been misconstrued; and the author's failure either to understand it or to give it a context amounts to a serious misrepresentataion of Black attitudes toward Jews.

Both Whitfield's critique and a reply by Dinnerstein in the same issue turn, in part, on whether stereotypes may be used positively as well as negatively, with Whitfield contending that they can and Dinnerstein holding to the position that "... stereotypes, both positive and negative, are unfair because they attribute uniform, and often inaccurate, characteristics to all individuals in a group. ..."

Compared to the larger question of Black anti-semitism, the existence of which both authors take for granted, a disagreement over whether stereotypes can be positive as well as negative or are unfair under either circumstance would seem to be the sort of issue that could arouse the passions only of scholars. In this instance, however, the disagreement is of substantive importance, for it reflects and affects profoundly—as the earlier review of the literature documents—the way in which a sizeable portion of recorded Black sentiment toward Jewish people has been read and interpreted for the past fifty years.

There are, in fact, a great number of statements, commentaries, and other writings by Black Americans that speak disparagingly of Jews. There are also numerous instances of statements by Black civil rights leaders, writers, and others that point to the Jewish community and its American experience (as well as its Biblical tradition) as a model worthy of emulation. The noted Black poet, James Weldon Johnson, is cited both by Dinnerstein and Whitfield as an example. On one occasion, Johnson noted the nation's Jewish populace and its experience as one from which Black Americans could "draw encouragement and hope." Regrettably, he chose to base his assertion on the spurious claim that the "two million Jews" in American exercised a "controlling interest in the finances of the nation."

Taken at face value, we might say that Johnson's motives were honorable, even if his facts were wrong. His intent appears clearly to be that of suggesting Black America could learn something of importance about economic power from the Jewish experience. This general sentiment about economic power in ethnic communities is not new; Johnson was neither the first nor the last to note it, and it is an issue discussed not only in relation to Jewish Americans but also and currently in cities like Detroit in relation to Chaldean Americans (who are stereotyped as "Arabs") and on the West Coast where it is considered to be a significant virtue of Asian communities. Nevertheless, we are left with the question of whether to give, in Johnson's case, greater weight to honest intent or inaccurate data. And under either circumstance, we are faced with the more serious issue of whether good motives and poor information add up to an example of Black anti-semitism.

In a similar vein, much of the other "incontrovertible evidence"—especially that from the period prior to the mid-1960s—must be assessed. Dinnerstein and Whitfield find themselves locked in dispute as to whether B. T. Washington and W. E. B. DuBois were closet anti-semites who modified their positions after their respective causes became the recipients of Jewish philanthropy and whether, in the case of Washington, he became pro-Jewish in public and remained anti-semitic in his private views. Horace Mann Bond, Richard Wright, James Baldwin, and Ralph Bunche have been subjects of similar analyses. In nearly all instances, the existence of Black anti-semitism is assumed; childhood memories as in the case of Bond and Wright, personal recollections such as those of James Baldwin, or public comments versus private correspondence as with Washington are given intense scrutiny, and decisions are reached regarding whether the claim of Black anti-semitism can be sustained or denied.

Nearly every analysis of any issue or problem begins not with the facts but with a set of stated or unstated assumptions. As Allport notes:

The human mind must think with the aid of categories (the term is equivalent to generalizations). Once formed, categories are the basis for normal prejudgment. We cannot possibly avoid this process. Orderly living depends on it. . . . A new experience *must* be redacted into old categories. We cannot handle each new event freshly in its own right. . . . Bertrand Russell . . . has summed up the matter in a phrase, 'a mind perpetually open will be a mind perpetually vacant.' (1954, pp. 19–20)

For scholars, assumptions are usually stated in the form of working hypotheses, which are then proven or disproven by whatever data or other information that can be assessed and presented as evidence. Nonscholars, but people for whom reason and reflection are important, go through essentially the same process in arriving at positions on issues or problems of consequence. They come to such matters not with a blank mental state but with a set of opinions based on personal values, prior experience, or ideological convictions. That which separates such individuals from the prejudiced and the bigoted is not that one avoids prejudgment while the other does not—clearly, both do—but that the former, unlike the latter, are willing to modify or change their prejudgments on the basis of evidence to the contrary.

When we come, therefore, to the issue of stereotypes, prejudice, and Black anti-semitism, a careful reading of the record would suggest caution—in the process of trying to determine the latter—before too much is made of stereotypical statements and commentaries. It would be folly to claim that stereotypes are inconsequential; it is also a serious error to insist that they are something more than they represent.

## II

The next order of complexity surrounds the question of whether recent disagreements between Black and Jewish leaders over civil rights goals and strategies have stained whatever positive images and reinforced certain negative perceptions that Black Americans traditionally have held of Jewish people. Here, the findings of the study on which this volume reports, while not definitive, are instructive.

The findings suggest that among Black Protestant churchgoers, a view of Jewish Americans as supportive of issues of civil rights and social justice still maintains, that Jewish people are not thought of in stereotypical terms such as "conceited", "unscrupulous," or "ruthless"; that they are not considered to be as prejudiced toward Black people as other white Americans; and that the image of "Jews-as-Christ-killers" is not salient among this group.

That these are the responses of Black Americans who are regular church attendees who report that religion plays an important part in their private, devotional life as well their public expression of religious commitment and whose church membership is to be found principally in historically Black Protestant denominations, is highly significant. It points first to a significant segment of the Black populace—more significant in numbers than any other category of analysis for identifying Black sentiment on issues—whose views toward the Jewish populace are not those expressed by anti-semites. Second, and against those who have opined on the subject, it suggests that historic Black Protestantism is not a salient source of anti-semitic beliefs among the Black populace. Third, it raises the possibility that whatever negative sentiments this group of respondents—and by extension the segment of the Black populace they represent—holds toward Jewish people need to be analyzed and understood in other than anti-semitic terms.

In undertaking such an analysis, it may be helpful to note that the current quarrel of Black America is not only with the nation's Jewish populace. From the mid-1950s to Martin Luther King, Jr.'s death, the plight of Black Americans was not only a principal item on the nation's public agenda, it commanded the attention of the private sector as well. The media reported continuously on the conditions of the nation's Black poor and on a segregated South, while private foundations directed millions of dollars into educational programs, social services, and new experiments designed to alleviate more than a century of postslavery neglect of a segment of the American populace to which many believed the nation had a unique obligation. Colleges and universities initiated special efforts to increase their enrollments of Black students and to establish academic programs that would enlighten future generations of young Americans regarding the particular history, culture, and contributions of the Black experience to American society. Corporations—some on their own initiative, others prodded by government legislation—moved to open up employment opportunities at increasingly higher levels to Black citizens.

The decade of the 1970s marked a slow but steady, discernible retreat from this national commitment to a long-overdue societal debt. Black America watched as the media, without the nightly dramas of encounters between marchers committed to nonviolence and unregenerate southern sheriffs dedicated to its opposite, found other issues to highlight. The nation's Black citizens observed private foundations shift their resources to other issues as well—the environment and feminism began to edge out civil rights and poverty as new philanthropic priorities. Colleges and universities, with a decade of nationwide effort to put under their social microscope, began to report that much of the prior decade's accomplishments on poverty and civil rights were subject to serious question, both with respect to objectives and outcomes. The nation's liberal community, sensing that it had done as much for the Black cause as the national mood would permit, turned its attention to the plight of other oppressed minorities—the handicapped, the gay community, and the mentally ill. Finally, political leaders, even more acutely aware of a conservative climate among the majority populace, began to counsel a course of benign neglect on the issue of race in America. Ironically, only in the private corporate sector did the breakthroughs of the 1960s in Black employment continue, albeit at a slower pace and in competition with the newer corporate conscience toward the employment of women.

For many Black Americans, therefore, the past twenty years have been an era of growing disenchantment with America's flagging commitment to racial justice. The disenchantment has been turned into embitterment in the past decade by a national administration that has not only questioned the merits of the past quarter-century's achievements in civil rights and equal opportunity but also set itself to the task of dismantling the legislative and judicial foundations on which that record has been built. If Black America currently has a quarrel, it is with a nation that has turned its back on a priority, which a generation ago seemed so clear and urgent. Rightly or wrongly, if Black America takes particular note of its past allies in the course of articulating its anger and in the process does so in ways that appear intemperate and ill-considered, it may reflect a recognition of the importance of that support in the past and a yearning to see it renewed in the present and for the future.

## III

A third order of complexity is raised by the question of whether the quarrel of Black Americans with the American Jewish community stems from the Black perception that American Jews have become more "American" than Jewish. It is a query suggested as early as 1948 in James Baldwin's "Harlem Ghetto" essay and has been repeated, periodically and in various forms, by Black writers and spokespersons ever since.

If it is a criticism of the American Jewish community, its intent, at the least, is a positive one. While it may be considered presumptuous for outsiders to point to a conflict of values within the Jewish community in America, the question is a firm but essentially friendly way of asking whether the Biblical Jewish tradition of social justice—of concern for the poor and the oppressed that consistently appears in conjunction with a radical challenge to wealth and power—may have become eclipsed by the ethic of American capitalism.

Such a question and its implicit criticism may be considered inappropriate or unfair, but such responses do not invalidate the question. It is clearly one for which this volume's survey offers no empirical evidence, either to affirm or deny the extent to which this may be a viewpoint held by Black Americans. The literature, however, suggests that it is and that it may be prominent particularly among those Black Americans who attach significance to the Biblical history and tradition of Jewish people.

Two historians, working on documents—in one instance that deal with Black-Jewish relations in a southern city during the period preceding the Civil War until just prior to World War I (Hertzberg, 1978) and, in the other, that examines on a wider scope the era at the turn of the century (Foner, 1975)—note this Black quandary. Hertzberg suggests that the advice of Black leaders to "imitate the Jews" was proffered with some ambivalence, particularly when direct experiences with Jewish individuals did not fulfil expectations. Specifically, when Black leaders encountered Jewish Americans who were not supportive of civil rights goals, the former would charge that the latter who also had been victims of slavery, oppression, and discrimination and who were expected to be the special heirs of the legacy of Biblical Judaism, "ought to know better." Foner found that Black leaders occasionally opined that their problem was not that Jews are Jewish but that they were not Jewish enough, that they "failed to live up to their own principles as exemplifed by Moses and the Prophets."

Whether or how frequently this ambivalent emulation theme is expressed currently is a matter of speculation. Among ideologues in the Black community, this idea has no currency whatsoever; it has been replaced by an insistence that Jewish America is a particular enemy of the Black cause. But the lack of salience of Black militant or nationalist sentiment among the nation's twenty-seven million Black citizens has been documented with sufficient frequency to suggest that, with the exception of its appeal to a younger segment of the Black populace, it would be highly unwise to make too much of this marginal attitude in the Black community.

For the overwhelming numbers of Black Americans, those who cling to a deep-rooted Christian faith and a belief in the American ideals of justice and equality, one may continue to expect that events and circumstances—both current and future—will cause them to question the commitments of other Americans to the latter ideals. It is a question that has been and will continue to be addressed to white America; if it is addressed to the American Jewish community, it is best understood also as a recognition of past comradeship based on a uniquely shared vision and as an expression of concern that such will not be lost for the future struggle.

There is one cluster of attitudes in the survey on which this volume reports that may be viewed with concern by many in the American Jewish community. Black Protestants appear to make a major distinction in their views toward Jewish people, per se, and those about Israel. Respondents tend to see Israel as "guilty of treating Palestinians in the same manner" that Jews themselves have received over the centuries and consider Israeli attitudes, rather than those of Arabs, to be the major obstacle to peace in the Middle East. At the same time, respondents view the Arabs as determined to drive the Israelis from "Palestine" and tend to support the right of the Israelis to defend their homeland. Finally, there is respondent agreement with the proposition that "Jews are more loyal to Israel than to America."

In the analysis and interpretation of these findings, it is important to note again that the survey from which they are taken was conducted in 1986, more than a year before the American press began to report at length on the Israeli government's response to Palestinian uprisings throughout Israel and before the recent Arab-Israeli peace initiative that has caused such a stir in the Western world. Whatever respondent attitudes reflect, therefore, are based on a lengthier set of perceptions than those that might arise from more recent events.

To the extent that they mirror a deep debate within Israel and among Israelis themselves—as well as within the American Jewish community—these attitudes should not be considered surprising. What they pose is yet another instance of a profound dilemma for the American Jewish community: how shall it view and respond to non-Jews who are critical of policies of the State of Israel, particularly with respect to its stance on the Palestinian issue?

The question is a complex one. For some in the American Jewish community, the issue is indivisible: to be pro-Jewish is to be pro-Israel or, stated conversely, any criticism of or lack of fervor for the State of Israel on the part of non-Jews inevitably betrays a latent, anti-Jewish and ultimately anti-semitic sentiment. For others in the Jewish community, the matter is not quite so stark: one may readily affirm the existence of the State of Israel, strongly defend its right to do so within secure borders, roundly condemn the avowed intent of segments of the Arab world to "drive the Israelis into the sea," and still reserve the right, for Jews and non-Jews alike, to raise concerns about or objections to specific Israeli government policies or practices.

For Christians of whatever hue, the issue is especially delicate. The Christian community has not been in the forefront of those who have made a clear, unambiguous affirmation on behalf of the State of Israel. While the record of theologically conservative Christian denominations, which includes those to which the re-

spondents in this survey adhere, is markedly better than that of
the liberal Protestant American camp, there are also reasons to
question some of the former's motives. Nevertheless, and for
whatever reason, if Christians are clear about the main issue (i.e.,
the right of the State of Israel to exist within secure borders and
to defend itself against acts of terrorism and other overt hostilities) then the corresponding right to dissent from specific Israeli
policies or acts of the Israeli government should be assumed.

The matter is made difficult for Christians, however, by what is
at base a Biblically romanticized view of Israel. Rather than seeing
the State of Israel as a tiny, relatively new nation, struggling for
survival in the midst of twentieth-century geopolitics, fending its
way between superpowers which view Israel as a strategic pawn in
a much larger game of global political chess, and faced with the
constant threat of warfare from several of its surrounding Arab
neighbors, together with the internal insecurity that an unrelenting experience with terrorism creates, a large swath of the Christian community wishes to see the modern state of Israel as a
reflection of the ancient Biblical motif of "a light unto the Gentiles."

Against every contemporary realism, many Christians would
like to think of Israel as above the political intrigues, the decep-
tions, and the games of power politics that every other modern
nation takes for granted as the norm in today's political world.
Somehow, among the pronouncements of a Peres, Shamir, or
Rabin, they listen for the prophetic voice of an Amos or Hosea,
calling the Israeli people to remember that a nation that is not
built on truth and justice cannot endure without the corresponding recognition that truth and justice in today's world lie some-
where between the moral passion of the ancient prophets and the
grim realities of a post-Holocaust, thermonuclear world.

The fact that the Biblical vision of Israel is debated more
fiercely among modern Israelis than anyone else is a matter for
respectful gratitude but not, as many Christians would do, for
seeking to hold Israel to a higher standard of conduct in its political affairs than any other modern nation-state. Israel is not entitled to special considerations on the scale of political norms;
neither can it be held by non-Israelis to higher rules of political

behavior than those to which the rest of the world is willing to subscribe.

Israel, however, for many Black Americans poses a special problem, one which is felt with no less intensity than that which Jewish Americans feel whenever their loyalty to America versus their commitment to Israel is questioned. If Jewish Americans feel a dual obligation toward the land of their people and that of their citizenship, so do many Black Americans. Regardless of whether the historical and geographical parallels are appropriate, many Black Americans feel themselves to be as deeply and emotionally invested in the struggle that has unfolded in South Africa as do Jewish Americans in the survival of Israel. Black Americans see the same essential issues at stake: the right of a people to inherit their homeland, to enjoy the privileges of citizenship in their own nation, secure against the hostility and oppression of forces that wish to drive them, if not into the sea, into a position of permanent servitude. For many Black Americans, the situation in South Africa at the present moment is similar, in a striking fashion, to that of Jews in Palestine in the years immediately preceding the formation of the State of Israel, when Jewish freedom-fighters used every means at their disposal to convince Britain that it must release its grip on their country and its people.

In the struggle for freedom and justice in South Africa, the record of the State of Israel, unfortunately, has been a checkered one. Israel conducts a lively economic relationship with the Republic of South Africa, which includes the sale of military materiels. Until recently, it refused to join most of the Western world in efforts to impose economic sanctions on South Africa. While few Western countries have clean hands with respect to the pariah nation that is South Africa, the stance of Israel—precisely because of its own history and that of its people—is viewed particularly by Black Americans as contradictory at best.

Further, the moral linkages between the most consuming issue for the Jewish people—the Holocaust—and that of apartheid is not lost on the modern Black conscience. The parallels are made continuously by Black Africans themselves: Archbishop and Nobel Peace Prize laureate Desmond Tutu made such an analysis in his closing address to an assembly in Seattle, Washington, in 1984;

Professor Kofi Opoku of the University of Ghana delivered a brilliant paper on "The Holocaust and Apartheid" at an international conference on Holocaust studies at Oxford in 1988. Both expressions are examples of a widespread concern at one level and considerable ambivalence at another toward a people whose uniquely painful history is assumed to give them an especial reason for sensitivity to the South African drama as the most urgent and compelling moral issue to be confronted in a post-Holocaust world.

In all of this, the effort herein is not to excuse or justify Black attitudes toward Israel but to display the current circumstances in which those attitudes arise and are expressed. If the American Jewish community wishes Black Americans to understand its apprehensions about Black attitudes toward Israel, Jewish citizens must come to terms with an equal set of misgivings on the part of many Black Americans regarding Israel's posture toward South Africa. Perhaps far more than disagreements on domestic policy issues, such as affirmative action, a significant part of the future of Black-Jewish relations in the United States may rest on how this question is addressed.

## IV

These foregoing considerations bring us to the final and, for this study, the most important question: whatever the expressed attitudes of Black Americans might be and whatever their source or ostensible justification, when they are all added up, do they constitute a Black chapter in the painful history of anti-semitism?

In one respect, the question is unanswerable. A half century of literature regarding this issue suggests that, in large measure, we are confronted with a mind-set that leads from immutable assumptions (e.g., that Black anti-semitism exists) to infallible, foregone conclusions. In this sphere, any statement critical of Jewish individuals or positions taken by Jewish organizations will be viewed as antisemitic cases-in-point.

Even at this level, however, it would be simplistic—and unwarrantably so—to suggest that anti-semitism, like beauty, is in the eye of the beholder. Extra-sensitivity to one's ethnicity, religion, or culture is not a uniquely Jewish trait.

Also, there is still a sufficient amount of documentable Black sentiment of a negative nature, expressed in negative stereotypes, distasteful stories, and prejudicial statements to warrant asking whether they equate with what we know to be the classical features and the characteristics of anti-semitism.

What we know regarding the phenomenon of anti-semitism can be summarized as follows. For those who have given serious study to the subject, anti-semites view Jewish people as a foreign, minority element that disturbs a society's homogeneity, that has international connections either to capitalism or communism, that poses a threat to the purity and order of mainstream society, and that serves as a scapegoat for society's ills, either real or imagined.[1]

All four of these themes or features appear wherever we can identify serious anti-semitic sentiments. They are clearly manifest in American society from its Populist period in the 1890s to the era of Henry Ford, Father Charles E. Coughlin, and the Reverend Gerald L. K. Smith. As early as 1837, one finds the governor of Mississippi, which had defaulted on its state bonds, blaming Baron Rothschild for having ". . . the blood of Judas and Shylock . . . in his veins" but it is in the Populist period that America's contribution to anti-semitism comes to full flower. As the late historian Richard Hofstadter writes:

> . . . it was chiefly Populist writers who expressed the identification of the Jew with the usurer and the 'international gold ring' which was the central theme of the American anti-Semitism of the age. . . . the frequent references to the House of Rothschild made it clear that for many silverites the Jew was an organic part of the conspiracy theory of history. (Hofstadter 1955, p. 78)

At the other end of this time frame, the anti-semitic notions of Henry Ford, a preeminent Populist, are well-known. Ford managed to combine a hatred for Wall Street with a hatred for the Jews that was repeatedly expressed in his publication, *The Dearborn Independent* and that made him a major source in the 1920s for the circulation of the infamous *Protocols of the Elders of Zion*, a work in which the four themes of anti-semitism are systematically set forth.

Ford's sentiments were matched, if not exceeded, by those of Gerald L. K. Smith and Father Charles Coughlin. Smith imbibed the Populist tradition during a pastorate in Louisiana and a subsequent post in the administration of Governor Huey "Kingfish" Long. By the end of World War II, Smith had earned himself the title of "dean of American Anti-Semitism" (Ribuffo 1983, p. 167).

It was an epithet Smith richly deserved. Both during the war and in his postwar writings and speeches, he became increasingly preoccupied with "the Jewish problem" and urged Jewish leaders to "shut up their troublemakers." He warned that it was dangerous for "aggressive members of the [Jewish] race to obtain too much power in government," considered the Anti-Defamation League to be a "Gestapo organization," and finally managed, in 1944, to run for the U.S. Presidency on the America First Party ticket and on a party platform that took specific note of "the Jewish problem," demanding that it be solved "honestly, realistically, and courageously." By 1948, Smith's newspaper, *The Cross and the Flag,* was consistently promoting the theme that Jewish communists were locked in a conspiracy with Jewish capitalists to gain world power.

If Smith is appropriately termed the dean of American anti-semitism, his associate in many of his endeavors—the famed radio priest, Charles Coughlin—ranks as dean of American fascists. Not only one of the principal disseminators of *The Protocols,* in 1938 Coughlin was reproducing and distributing the anti-semitic propaganda of Julius Streicher, Nazi Gauleiter of Franconia, founder of the anti-semitic journal *Der Sturmer,* and one of the leading Jew-haters of the Nazi period. Coughlin was a key speaker at the first mass meeting of American Nazis, held in Madison Square Garden in 1939, and his organization, the Christian Front, was responsible for the severe beatings of Jews in several American cities.

In these several examples, we are given a view of anti-semitism in American life that is matched by the likes of the Reverend Richard Butler and his followers in the present period. Their themes are the same: the Jews as an unwelcome and unwanted minority, engaged in political and financial conspiracy either to control capitalism or advance communism (or, as in the case of Smith, to manage somehow both feats simultaneously), who threaten the purity of American life and are responsible for most, if not all, of its ills.

These are also the major themes of European anti-semitism

that the Nazis developed and enlarged into its most extreme forms. There, as the eminent scholar Franz Neumann wrote during the war:

> ... there is hardly a book, a pamphlet, or an ideological pronouncement that does not attack Jewish conspiracy, Jewish immorality, the Jewish disintegrating spirit, Jewish capitalism, Jewish rationalism, Jewish pacifism, Jewish militarism. There is almost no vice that is not attributed to Jews. (1944, p. 124)

It was this pervasive, collective set of sentiments that permitted what Neumann terms the "totalitarian Anti-Semite" to rise to the fore—the person for whom "the Jew has long ceased to be a person (and) . . . has become the reincarnation of evil." This became the seedbed of Nazi government policy that led to the death camps and mass extermination.

If these are the characteristics and expressions of classical anti-semitism, one must strain—and the outcome will be unsuccessful—to find them in Black America, either in the past or in the present. Their manifestation in the pronouncements of Louis Farrakhan are acknowledged and their echo in earlier writings and statements of a very few who wished or presumed to speak for Black Americans can be documented. But the fact that the nation's Black populace has repudiated these sentiments consistently—that those who espouse them have failed to attract any significant following among Black people in the United States—stands as clear a questioning of the claim of Black anti-semitism as could be made. If the claim is to have validity, some evidence that it exists in the virulent form described above and among a significant portion of the nation's twenty-seven million Black citizens needs to be presented. No such evidence exists.

It may be asked legitimately, in considering this analysis and avowal, whether anti-semitism has been raised to such a level of specificity that its manifestations are narrowed and isolated only to their most virulent forms. The answer depends on whether one's interests are inclined toward analysis or assertion. Knowing the inhuman ends to which anti-semitism in any form can lead, there is every reason to attempt a careful diagnosis of its multiple forms and antecedents. Such attempts, in the process, should seek to specify those individual or collective conditions that may lead, demonstrably, to aggressive Jewish-hatred and not confuse them with sentiments, however distasteful, which do not reflect this defining, essential quality of anti-semitism. We should especially avoid such a sweeping claim as "Black anti-semitism," which denotes the very same process of categorization and condemnation that the term itself seeks to denounce.

## V

For most readers, a discussion of Black Protestantism and anti-semitism would not be complete, particularly in this period, without addressing the phenomenon of the Reverend Jesse Jackson who, in his meteoric rise to national prominence and his commanding presence in American politics, came to symbolize, in many quarters in the Jewish community, fears regarding Black anti-semitism. The outcome of his bid for nomination as the Democratic Party's 1988 presidential candidate notwithstanding, Jackson will remain a powerful voice and force on the national scene. His views on any topic and, in the context of this discussion, on Jewish Americans and issues that they hold dear, are not, therefore, inconsequential.

Jesse Jackson was born barely two months before Pearl Harbor and the United States' entry into the Second World War and less than six months before the infamous Wannsee Conference at which the plans for Nazi Germany's "final solution of the Jewish question" were put into motion. Both the Holocaust and the war were ended before Jackson entered kindergarten.

Jackson's experiences and the views and values that they have engendered have been shaped, therefore, by a postwar, post-Holocaust world. He grew to manhood in a period in which the Black struggle for justice was reaching its heights; he was fourteen when Rosa Parks refused to yield her seat on a Montgomery bus to a white passenger, in his early twenties when the United States Congress passed a succession of key civil rights acts, and twenty-six when Martin Luther King, Jr. was assassinated. His formative years were influenced by an era of immense hope, followed by a period of keen disappointment in the civil right movement in America.

By the time Jackson reached his thirties, the Grand Alliance between Black and Jewish leaders already had begun to unravel. The mood in Black America was one of self-determination and the stance in the Jewish community, in response, was one of withdrawal and criticism. Black nationalist rhetoric was at its peak in the late 1960s and early 1970s; how much of this sentiment Jackson imbibed is debatable, but its impact on a generation of young Black leaders is undeniable. Integrationist sentiments among Black leaders were being seriously challenged, and attempts to fill the leadership vacuum were being made by a large number of claimants, all of whom had to contend with a fragmented Black agenda, the loss of organizational support from once staunch allies, and the discernible conservatism of the political climate in the nation.

If efforts to explain are not confused with or distorted into attempts to excuse, these three factors likely provide the fairest, most objective circumstances within which to access Jesse Jackson. His memories are not of the war and the calamity that befell European Jewry during its midst. His experiences are not those of the era of Black-Jewish cooperation but rather those that occurred after the alliance between leaders of the two communities had broken down. He has come into prominence in a period in which Black and Jewish leaders have established their separate agendas, and Jackson, unlike the Black political philosophy and assumptions that preceded him, has chosen to give powerful articulation to a different set of needs based on a new set of realities that today confront the majority of the nation's Black populace.

Black leaders, virtually since the Civil War, have been torn between an approach to white America that would focus on opportunities for those Black citizens prepared to take advantage of them versus an appeal to address the conditions of the nation's Black masses. Essentially and greatly condensed, this was the nub of the famed disagreement between W. E. B. DuBois and Booker T. Washington. At the leadership level of Black America, throughout most of this century, it has been the DuBois philosophy that has prevailed: a challenge to the nation and an insistence that it permits educated, competent, motivated Black men and women to enter college, hold jobs, buy homes, participate in the political process, and enjoy all the other perquisites of citizenship that the rest of society claims. For well over a half century, the legal strategies of the NAACP, the programs of the National Urban League, the appeals of the United Negro College Fund, and the efforts of innumerable Black fraternal, social, and cultural organizations have rested on this essentially DuBoisian philosophy.

Jesse Jackson has come to prominence in a period in which this appeal, while still subscribed to by millions of Black Americans, no longer addresses adequately the plight of a significant segment of the Black populace. The countless millions of Black poor who seemingly are destined permanently to be so; the Black men whom the economists benignly term the "underemployed" and the "permanently unemployable;" Black families caught in a cycle of public assistance; the Black teenage unwed mother; the Black youngsters caught in the vise of the drug traffic, either as victims or entrepreneurs—this is the portion of Black America to which Jackson began making an appeal almost twenty years ago and the segment from which he has received his most enthusiastic response.

As American society has come increasingly to divide itself between the privileged and the permanently poor and, particularly, as the prevailing political rhetoric of the 1980s has found it plausible to blame the latter for their own circumstances, Jackson has discovered that his message reaches the ears not only of the nation's disadvantaged Black populace but also increasing numbers of other Americans who find themselves in the same set of socioeconomic conditions. Jackson today is being welcomed and warmly received by white coal miners in Virgina, victims of plant closures in Wisconsin, beleaguered farmers in Iowa, and countless others for whom the American Dream is no longer a realistic possibility.

In the course of his career, Jackson has taken positions and expressed sentiments that create concern in some quarters of the American Jewish community, cause alarm in others, and evoke bitter resentment among still others. His embrace of Arafat in 1979 and his connection with Farrakhan in 1984 have been noted, along with his regrettable "Hymie Town" remarks. Whatever his posture in 1984 on issues sensitive to the Jewish community, Jackson has done his best to overcome the estrangement his stance created. In 1988, he distanced himself from Farrakhan to a degree that was astonishing for a political candidate who would normally have wished to avoid alienating any potential constituency. He did not repeat the error of making anti-Jewish slurs. He has attempted to address, with candor, his views toward the Middle East, Israel, and the volatile issue of the Palestinians.

It is not the purpose of this essay to defend Jesse Jackson's ideas or viewpoints. Nevertheless, with respect to the serious problems that rage in the Middle East, it is worth noting that Jackson expresses, in unequivocal terms, Israel's right to exist within secure borders and his support for the United Nations resolution that affirms this principle. He is equally unequivocal in his insistence on the issue of a homeland for the Palestinians and on the need for Israel to address this problem. Whether one agrees with his stance or not, his argument that the Israelis give up portions of their conquered territories for such a purpose is no more than that advanced by the secretary of state in the Reagan administration.

On relationships between Black and Jewish Americans, Jackson's comments are especially relevant. He sees the source of the current friction as "a power transition" that is taking place. His examples, perhaps dictated by the setting in which his observations were made (*New York Times* interview, 16 April 1988) reflect the unfortunate tendency to depict Black-Jewish relations nationally in the light of events and circumstances in New York City. Nevertheless, he describes the current tension as ". . . based on a struggle of adjusting our (i.e., Black-Jewish) relationship" and speaks of ". . . the advantage of (Black-Jewish) mutual growth and development."

Jesse Jackson's views are subject to challenge and debate. His stature as a political leader is enormous and, to the extent that he expresses the deep concerns, disappointments, and hopes of a growing segment of the American populace, is deserved. But to return once again to the theme of this volume, it is Jesse Jackson as a Black Protestant minister that, in the final analysis, is most significant.

Like generations of Black clerics before him and undoubtedly many who will follow, Jackson holds a unique position in Black America. He is, in one and the same moment, preacher, educator, prophet, social commentator, and articulator of the moods, aspirations, and grievances of his people. He expresses in his rhetoric the cadences of a religious tradition on which Black Americans in great numbers have thrived for over a century. His message is deeply rooted in the Hebraic-Christian vision of justice in the world. He embodies both the hopes (in his claim that regardless of one's background one can achieve in this nation) and the fears (that because he is Black, he will not be taken seriously) of an inordinate number of citizens in our society.

For the American Jewish community, therefore, it would be well to take Jesse Jackson seriously, not just for himself but for the new generation of Black leadership that he symbolizes. The prospect of returning to an era similar to that of the Grand Alliance in Black-Jewish relations is not great; Jackson's call for an "adjustment" in Black-Jewish relations is long overdue.

But on the most optimistic note possible, Jackson's rise to national prominence suggests that Black leadership is still drawn from a tradition heavily influenced by religious sentiments and convictions. The strong Hebraic foundations of that tradition offer continued and even new possibilities for Black-Jewish understanding and effort. It is these possibilites that Black and Jewish citizens, in concert, have a mutual, vested interest in advancing, lest there arise future generations of Pharaohs "who knew not Joseph. . . ."

# 5

## Epilogue
## Black Anti-Semitism:
## The Rationality of Oppression

### LYMAN H. LEGTERS

Early in 1948 an aspiring novelist, James Baldwin, published in *Commentary* an essay entitled "The Harlem Ghetto." This was just before Baldwin left the United States to work on the novel that became *Go Tell It On the Mountain*. Because he was not yet famous and because his essay was written in such a way as to leave open the question of the author's color, readers had no reason to associate his remarks about Black anti-semitism with his personal experience, except in so far as he exhibited a resident's familiarity with Harlem and a Black man's deep feeling for the problems of what was then still called the Negro world.

The concluding section of the essay, in which Baldwin addressed the issue of Black sentiments toward Jews, underscores the ambiguity of the relationship between two peoples who were in some measure covictims of the bigotry surrounding them in the majority population. Although the essay was cast more in terms of personal attitudes than of socioeconomic relations, there was appropriate attention given to the economic position of Jews in Harlem. Despite the principal inhabitants' awareness of covictimization and despite the habit of looking to their covictims for succor and some leadership in the struggle against oppression, Jews as landlords and shopkeepers also figured in Black consciousness as immediate and very visible representatives of an oppressive white social order. A Jew who stood for exploitation in Harlem might have a brother leading the campaign against social discrimination; conceivably they might even be the same person.

In a seminar on modern protest literature, I recently had occasion to query students about their reactions to Baldwin's essay. Their experience, I had to remind myself, stood about as far this side of the civil rights struggle as the essay lay on the other side. The responses, in any case, were prompt and completely contradictory. Some saw James Baldwin as an apologist for anti-semitism; others saw his essay as a legitimate exercise in explanation. One set of respondents regarded anti-semitism as a uniform and, of course, inexcusable phenomenon, perhaps reflecting a certain kind of post-Holocaust thinking in which all anti-semitism leads inexorably to a genocidal outcome. The second group understood anti-semitism as multiform, deplorable in all of its manifestations yet also subject to differentiation according to circumstances, some of which may have rational explanatory value.

Since the latter view is also my own, I want to suggest why some manifestations of anti-semitism may be more understandable than others; why, more specifically, I regard the factor of oppression as one that must be taken into account in any nuanced understanding of anti-semitism. I should not have to add but will anyway: it is not a matter of finding excuses for particular expressions of anti-semitism, but rather, while recognizing that even the mildest forms may nurture the murderous kind, of acknowledging that not all forms are equally murderous. For only such a discriminating view will sustain the effort to combat particular manifestations in appropriate ways.

An earlier analogue to the Harlem situation of James Baldwin's description occurred in the nineteenth-century working class of Europe. Here I refer not so much to the ideological spokesmen for the working class—Bakunin or Proudhon, for example—who displayed anti-semitic tendencies, but rather to the attitudes of rank-and-file, among whom the appearance of anti-Jewish sentiment could mirror either the widespread popular bigotry endemic in several European populations or a specific consciousness of capitalist exploitation of workers. In the latter case, resentment of particular employers and financial magnates seems to have gone hand in hand and on a rising curve with the growing realization that the disadvantaged state of the working class was not a natural and inescapable condition but one rooted either in an evil system or in individual villainy and, hence, susceptible of being changed. Whichever causal analysis obtained and whether suspicion or concerted action was the chosen instrument of change, an enemy had appeared to supplant fate or destiny as the reason for misery. And it happened, not infrequently, that the enemy was either a Jew or the Jews. If the former, then it was no different from Marx's fulminations against Jewish financiers who propped up the hated vestiges of absolutism. Jews were in fact bankers and employers and might be the object of legitimate working class animosity. If the latter, however, then it was what August Bebel had in mind in speaking of the socialism of fools, a mistaken, simple-minded, and assuredly irrational and bigoted slide from a particular fact to a harmful generalization.

However mild or even benign such generalities might seem alongside the virulent and active forms current in other sectors of society, it was harmful in two senses: it harmed the proletarian cause by misidentifying the source of the problem and it was a sentiment available for mobilization in behalf of social purposes as far from being benign as they were from the interests of the working class. It is in this sense that condemnation of anti-semitism may safely be general and undifferentiated.

To complete the analogy between an awakening working class in nineteenth-century Europe and a newly articulate Harlem populace, it is necessary to notice the other dimension of the equation. In Europe also there was a consciousness of covictimization, a sense in which the working class could regard Jews as sympathizers at least and sometimes as allies. Again there was the Jewish record of advocacy of forward-looking reforms, animated no doubt by their own struggle for equality as citizens but potentially beneficial as well to other disadvantaged segments of any given population. More palpably, and this feature grew in scope as one looked from west to east, Jewish members of the working class underscored a congruence of interest that found expression in the overrepresentation of Jews in socialist and revolutionary movements, in the formations like the Bund in Poland and Russia, and in branches of social movements such as labor Zionism. So once again the relationship is ambiguous, ranging from substantial identity of interest and sentiment to a mythic identification of Jews with a system of exploitation.

It is not necessary to elaborate the analogy further, or to find others of similar character, to make the point: anti-semitism, always deplorable and dangerous, embraces a variety of motivations and expressive forms. It is *ipso facto* irrational for the person or persons holding such a belief, but some of the varieties of anti-semitism permit of rational explanation. Oppression, I submit, is such a perfectly rational explanation. It does not, to repeat, excuse this or any other form of primitivism, but the awareness that oppressed people often lash out thoughtlessly against fancied adversaries can make an otherwise irrational sentiment rationally understandable. It is impossible to say with perfect certainty whether one of Bebel's Social Democratic workers or one of Baldwin's Harlem neighbors is reflecting oppression or is merely a garden-variety anti-semite, but that does not invalidate the proposition that a good deal of the anti-semitism in both situations is made understandable by the experience of oppression.

These observations are perhaps not overwhelmingly interesting in themselves, but they lead to an implication of considerable consequence. If oppression can help to account for some portion of the anti-semitism abroad in the world, be it Black or any other variety, then that aspect of anti-semitism is fundamentally different from the variety sometimes known as racial. The difference is that it has an available social remedy, namely, the removal of the oppression. This remedy does not harm the Jew or even require, as Christian society has required, that he deny his faith, nor does it depend on tinkering with the psyche of the bigot. The removal of oppression simply rescinds the victim's impulse to strike out against visible and often merely symbolic representatives of the oppressive system. I do not mean to suggest that the struggle to remove oppression is ever easy or wholly successful, but that effort is at least a humane and positive one. It stands in marked contrast to the sometimes ugly and politically dangerous measures required to combat the kind of anti-semitism animated by racial and religious bigotry. Furthermore, and very significantly, the struggle against oppression may rekindle the awareness of covictimization by enlisting both sets of victims in a common effort that holds promise for both. Something of that sort seems to have occurred frequently in radical movements for social change, especially in Central and Eastern Europe, where—even if mistakenly—the campaign to eliminate exploitation and to transcend the primitivism of anti-semitism was regarded as a single joint struggle.

But what, it may be asked, does all of this have to do with an inquiry that has disclosed only negligible reservoirs of anti-Jewish sentiment in selected Black communities? Even if oppression is accepted as a conditioning factor helpful in explaining certain manifestations of anti-semitism and pointing to its eradication, why should the Black populace of the United States, which largely shares the experience of both systemic and personal oppression, not display an equally widespread and evenly distributed tissue of anti-semitic attitudes? From this perspective, it might be argued that the inquiry *should* have found signs of the particular anti-semitism we call Black distributed throughout its sample populations.

Unless we want to conclude that Black anti-semitism does not exist, and there is abundant evidence to counter such a conclusion, then we are left with the disquieting notion that a variety of anti-semitism specifically linked to the shared experience and/or memory of Black Americans appears in some circumstances but not in others. If, as I have argued, oppression is a specific feature of that linkage, then we still have to account for differential manifestations of the sentiment in question.

Both the European working class analogy and the James Baldwin essay seem to me to offer some illumination. We are of course not considering here the sense in which the working class or the Black American population simply reflect anti-semitic attitudes endemic in the larger population (as, in the corresponding case, we would not be considering Jewish reflections of common white prejudice). But if the modifiers are to have meaning, then the anti-semitism peculiar to Black Americans (or to the working class) must be accounted for in specific ways.

The first, it seems to me, is the availability of a palpable target of animosity, a Jewish landlord or banker or employer, who functions as a kind of lightening rod to focus anger on the perpetrators of injustice (who happen also to be Jewish). We do not typically ask of victims that they engage in rational analysis about relative numbers of Jewish oppressors or about a system of which particular Jews are merely accidental representatives. Rather, we understand the ugly delusion as a byproduct of oppression.

We also recognize it as a sign of desperation. The victims of oppression commonly undergo two awakenings: the realization that oppression is not a natural condition and the recognition that the means of concerted action may be used to overcome it. But if, having undergone this second awakening, the workers of a plant in Manchester or Baldwin's Harlem neighbors discover that the means of redress promised them by the formal rules of the social order are denied them in actuality, then they are at least encouraged to strike out unreasoningly and unreasonable against the palpable villains closest to hand.

Finally, we know that this kind of irrational response can be cushioned and attenuated by the consolations supplied to members of a community of victims. Even the community of the slave quarters provided such consolation. Black congregations have done so ever since, and so did the early working class associations that were fraternal more than they were instruments of struggle. Beyond the function of consolation, these communities—congregations, unions, enbryonic political parties—also channel discontent along strategic lines, thereby replacing irrational outbursts with rational calculation, whether the upshot is concerted action or acquiescence. At best they also counteract the possibilities of demagoguery, which has been so prominent in giving voice to both working class and Black anti-semitic sentiments that might otherwise have remained unspoken.

Place in this context, the phenomenon of Black anti-semitism can at once be understood and deplored, but above all it can be anticipated as an expression of quite specific circumstances. The communities examined in this investigation, among the least likely to display the special feature of Black anti-semitism, may thus be seen as the norm in our society but without denying either the actuality or the destructive potential of that phenomenon when circumstances allow it to flourish.

# Postscript

Writing on contemporary themes or "current history" has the advantage of focusing attention on topics that are fresh and of interest; the disadvantage lies in the difficulty of bringing the discussion to closure. There is always a more recent event or published work that ostensibly warrants analysis or, at the least, notation; failure to do so invites the sanction of sceptics and other critics anxious to pronounce a study as flawed or incomplete.

A book that attempted to discuss every salient event or development in the saga of Black-Jewish relations or every putative act of Black anti-semitism would never be published. In this instance, although the stream of literature on both topics has not subsided, the Dinnerstein-Whitfield debate (1986) has been taken as an arbitrary but appropriate point at which to conclude references to published studies and commentaries; little that is either new or substantive has been said regarding the issue since that time.

Since 1986, however, the clashes and conflicts between Black and Jewish Americans have continued to mount and, in the eyes of many members of the Jewish community, have become incontrovertible proof of the phenomenon of Black anti-semitism. Two articles in the 3 September 1991 edition of the *New York Times* display the difficulty in attempting dispassionate discussions of the issue. The first, a news story, reports on the annual West Indian–American Parade in Brooklyn in which "more than a million Black Caribbean–Americans marched, danced, shimmied and sang through troubled Crown Heights . . . in a chaotic, glorious cacophony of steel drums, reggae, rum and costumes that seemed to blast away much of the racial tensions plaguing the Brooklyn neighborhood."

Two weeks earlier, on 19 August, Crown Heights had been the scene of a double tragedy. An automobile, driven by a member of the Crown Heights Hasidic Jewish community, had run a stoplight, jumped a curb, and killed a seven-year-old Black child. The following day, in an apparent act of revenge, a Hasidic rabbinical student visiting from Australia was stabbed to death; a sixteen-year-old Black youth subsequently was arrested and charged with the murder. For days on end, the community remained a tinder-box. The parade, therefore, in which the mayor's office skillfully negotiated an arrangement that found six leaders of the Hasidic community accompanying Mayor Dinkins as parade Grand Marshall was seen by many as a welcomed sign that the worst of the recent community tensions had subsided, even if momentarily.

The September 3rd edition of the *New York Times* also carried a column by A. M. Rosenthal ["On My Mind"] headlined "Pogrom in Brooklyn." Almost as if the parade had not occurred or that the mayor and his staff had not spent almost every evening of the preceding two weeks on the streets of Crown Heights trying to restore calm and order or that there had not been an endless series of meetings among numerous Black and Jewish civic groups seeking to avert an escalation of the conflict, the Rosenthal column warned American Jews that ". . . the same kind of street thugs [will be led] to burn Jewish property and break Jewish bones in other cities" and denounced the "self destructiveness" of "influential prominent Black Americans . . . who do not understand or are not willing to say out loud that Crown Heights can do more damage to blacks than to Jews."

As most Americans know, the *New York Times* is not simply Metropolitan New York's morning daily. It is, by most accounts, the nation's premier newspaper, influential far beyond the confines of the five boroughs of New York City and read, perhaps, by more people who live outside the proverbial Big Apple than those who are its residents. When one of its columnists depicts the Crown Heights event as "an anti-Semitic pogrom" while a news story three days earlier reports that "mainstream Jewish organizations have begun to call the racial violence in Crown Heights a dangerous manifestation of anti-Semitism and not just a product of local Hasidic-black tensions," a local tragedy begins to take on national significance. This elevation of local news to national prominence and the implication that local attitudes displayed therein are to be found all across the country is, at one and the same moment, the story of contemporary discussions of anti-semitism and Black

America, as well as the reason that dispassionate discussions of the issue are so inordinately difficult to undertake.

# I

"Troubled Crown Heights" is home to a potpourri of ethnic groups. Two of those groups—one Black, the other Jewish—stand apart from the mainstreams of the communities with which they are nominally identified. Both groups are composed largely of immigrants, relatively recent in their arrival and participation in American life, compared to the larger ethnic communities of which they are a part. With their separate experiences of social isolation and thrown together in the same neighborhood in New York by circumstances neither group would likely choose, these two groups are part of a volatile demographic mixture in Crown Heights that has increasingly become a recipe for racial and ethnic disaster.

Brooklyn, the borough in which Crown Heights is situated, is thought to have the largest West Indian population in the world outside the Caribbean islands themselves. Almost one-half or 308,000 of New York's 668,000 West Indians live in Brooklyn; 85 percent of the Crown Heights populace is estimated to be Black or Hispanic, with many of the Black residents of Caribbean descent. The West Indians are as distinct in culture and life-style from New York's Black American populace as are the Hasidim from the city's Jewish residents.

The Hasidim of Crown Heights, in turn, are as different from the mainstream of the American Jewish community as West Indians are from America's Black populace. The Lubavitcher Hasidim are a cluster of ultraconservatism within what is already one of the most orthodox of Jewish religious movements. Founded in Lithuania in 1773, the Lubavitch-Chabad movement, as it is formally termed, was brought to the United States by its sixth leader, the Grand Rebbe, in 1940. The movement's headquarters were established on Eastern Parkway in the Crown Heights section of Brooklyn where they have become the "hub of the Lubavitch empire."

Crown Heights, therefore, has become home to two ethnic groups, both of which stand apart from the larger ethnic communities to which outsiders would nominally assign them. Each group has clashed repeatedly with the other; both groups clash constantly with other ethnic strands in Crown Heights: West Indians with Koreans, Hasidim with Latinos and Puerto Ricans. Susan Hartman, a Crown Heights resident, describes what takes place in this tumultuous community as "not symbolic of a racial war or even of a battle. It's part of a complicated—and only sometimes hostile—dance that goes on daily among the dozens of different ethnic groups hoping to get along and do business together."

If Crown Heights is a symbol of anything, it is the increasing inability of American society, in the third century of her democratic experiment, to acculturate the tides of today's immigrants as once she did. New York is the national emblem of assimilation in the United States. Not only has it served as the major port of entry for millions of new arrivals to this country, many of those arrivals stayed in the city that first welcomed them and became part of a succession of success stories of transformed Euro-Americans.

The older immigration experience was not free of conflict. Ethnic groups that had often warred with one another in southern and eastern Europe found themselves in competition and rivalry for living space and economic opportunity in the New World. But each wave of new arrivals struggled to find its niche in the turbulence that was American society, especially between 1880 and 1920; the goal for each group was to become quickly absorbed in, not to stand outside of, the new national life and culture.

What was once a process of succession has become an arena of conflict between groups who either choose to remain apart from the larger society, as in the case of the Lubavitcher Hasidim, or who find the larger society still hostile to their presence, as with the West Indian community. In the constant struggle for survival, the groups either compete for scarce public resources—as the Hasidim and the West Indians have for years—or view with hostility the arrival of immigrant groups who land even later and who appear to quickly overtake and pass them on the economic ladder, as the West Indians view the Korean and Palestinian merchants.

In such a racial and ethnic tinderbox, sparks fly constantly and conflagrations are regrettably all-too-frequent. The question is not whether incidents and expressions of anti-semitism are heard in Crown Heights and from persons who are Black; tragically, they do and are. At issue is whether such incidents and expressions are reflective of a set of attitudes around the nation that can accurately or properly be called "Black anti-semitism."

## II

Those who insist the attitudes displayed in Crown Heights are symptomatic of Black attitudes nationwide point to other phenomena as cases in point. One is the pronouncements of an African-American member of the faculty of City University of New York, Dr. Leonard Jeffries. Jeffries has come to prominence for tinging Afrocentrism—a quite respectble intellectual movement among some Black scholars—with dashes of anti-semitism and an assortment of other hatreds; he has been quoted as attributing the financing of the slave trade as well as Black stereotypes in Hollywood productions to Jewish wealth and influence. Jeffries and a few like-minded academics occasionally appear on some college campuses across the nation where their presentations cause considerable and understandable distress in the local Jewish communities where they are heard.

There is a brief list of names that also emerges whenever Black anti-semitism is discussed. It is headed by the Reverend Al Sharpton and the Reverend Herbert Daughtry, two New York City clergymen who manage to appear on the scene wherever Black-white and especially Black-Jewish conflicts occur. When added to the Farrakhan phenomenon, the impression grows in the American Jewish community that the whole of Black America has become a sink of anti-semitism.

Minister Farrakhan's views on Judaism and the Jewish people are well-known. He has been known to refer to Judaism as a "gutter religion" and to express, in other contexts, his admiration for Adolf Hitler. Following a media blitz in the spring of 1990 during which Mr. Farrakhan gave interviews to several Washington, D.C., newspapers and appeared on national television talk shows, speculation arose that he was intent on softening his image. He expressed his desire to "dialogue" with whites and even with Jews, insisting that his "gutter religion" comment had been a reference not to Judaism but to Israel's treatment of Palestinians (see "Critic's Notebook," *New York Times* March 29, 1990, B4).

What do these events and personages have in common? Beyond their evident dislike for Jewish people, these are all—with the single exception of Farrakhan—local New York phenomena. It is quite unlikely that nine out of ten Black Americans across the nation, if asked to identify Jeffries, Sharpton, or Daughtry, would know who they are. Farrakhan has a much higher public profile, but his sphere of influence remains remarkably limited; membership figures of the Nation of Islam are closely guarded, but they are estimated to be less than 1 percent of the nation's Black populace.

What remains is the Reverend Jesse Jackson and his long-standing image in the American Jewish community as the veritable symbol of Black anti-semitism. It is an image that Jackson cannot seem to shake, no matter how diligently he tries. Barely two weeks before the eruption in that city, Jackson gave a speech in Los Angeles that essentially was a message of reconciliation to the American Jewish community. It called upon Jewish and Black Americans to work together again, to try to repair the political bonds between the two communities that shaped so much of the history of civil rights and social justice in the United States.

Jackson spoke of fascism as a common threat to Jewish and Black people alike; he warned of the influence of David Duke and Patrick Buchanan on the American political agenda. He asserted that if he had caused pain himself to the nation's Jewish community, he would seek atonement, redemption, and renewal.

A. M. Rosenthal, cited earlier, subsequently recounted Jackson's Los Angeles speech as one that should be given attention "by his admirers and opponents" alike. Terming it "important and underreported," Rosenthal nevertheless made clear his skepticism about Jackson's genuineness. Almost simultaneously and in the midst of the Presidential primary in New York, former California Governor Jerry Brown offered to share the ticket with Jesse Jackson, a move that engendered modest support from Black voters and a disastrous loss of support among Jewish voters whose leaders in New York repeatedly condemned Brown's choice and his judgment.

## III

A century that opened with such promise in the relationships between Black and Jewish Americans threatens to close with those relations at an unprecedented low point. If this disintegration occurs in the accord between two peoples who shared for the better part of this century a common commitment to justice in America, it will be one of the major social tragedies of the modern era in this nation. But as the century draws to a close, lamenting a lost past is not likely to be as useful as examining whether a more positive and productive future is possible.

If it is, several things have to happen. First is the recognition that the Grand Alliance, as noted earlier, was one primarily between the national leaders of the Black and Jewish communities. This time, if it is to be renewed, the alliance must be built from the ground up, not from the top down. It must be a grass-roots effort in communities all across America where Black and Jewish citizens join hands in addressing specific, local issues of injustice.

Second, there needs to be an acknowledgment in both communities that Jesse Jackson is right in his call, not only for Black and Jewish citizens to work together but in identifying the common threat that both communities face. Such an acknowledgment on the part of Black citizens will oblige us to admit that much of the rhetoric in our community in the late 1960s was simply and tragically wrong. We cannot—as we were being urged to do a quarter century ago by a generation of radicalized leadership—go it alone. We need allies in the struggle for justice and turning again to one of our oldest allies is both sensible and long overdue.

Jewish acknowledgment will oblige abandoning Jesse Jackson as a lightening rod for Jewish anger or frustration over the state of Black-Jewish relations. It will oblige our Jewish colleagues to accept the fact that, unlike the protocol that governed the old alliance, Black leaders today may well express political views that are not endorsed in Jewish circles, and vice versa. A mature, in contrast to a paternalistic, relationship will search for that common ground and agenda on which both communities can agree, rather than continue to feud over issues that represent honest disagreements.

When the first two efforts have taken place, Black America should be ready to admit that we have a serious problem with some in our midst who hate Jews, while the Jewish community should be prepared to state that the incessant drumbeat about Black anti-semitism exacerbates rather than ameliorates the problem. Black leadership—political, religious, business, and civic—is painfully aware today that there is a segment of Black America that is predominantly young, alienated from nearly everything except its own generation, essentially ignorant of the Black struggle of the past, and disdainful of many of the values that most Black Amerians cherish. This is the segment of our populace that is the most visible casualty of postindustrial America; many were born after the assassination of Martin Luther King, Jr., and are products of poor inner-city schools from which those who do graduate are unable to find worthwhile jobs. This is the generation of young Black Americans who face a chronic situation of economic and social despair; there is also a small circle of Black voices that speaks to this generation, regrettably often in anti-semitic terms.

Blaming Jews for Black ills is only one of the many problems this group of Black Americans presents. As is so often the case where anti-semitism is found, hatred of Jews is accompanied by a hatred of the larger society, by the imagining of a mythic past of racial superiority—in this instance, Black racial supremacy—and by the conviction that violent social change is inevitable. Such attitudes are not simply wrong-headed; they are dangerous in any society, especially one that has proven to be as vulnerable as is ours to violent upheavals.

These attitudes, however, should not be confused with those of the mass of Black America or projected onto the entire populace as the unfortunate use of the term "Black anti-semitism" does. The term gives rise to the unwarranted impression that hatred of the Jews is widespread among Black Americans. It confuses those anti-semitic outbursts that do occur with a range of other expressions and attitudes that can be heard occasionally or even frequently in Black communities about Jewish people.

It is because Jewish citizens are so acutely aware of and sensitive to the consequences of such attitudes that many are inclined to respond immediately and vigorously to any negative expressions about Jews as signs of anti-semitism. But precisely because the consequences of anti-semitism have proven to be so uniquely horrendous, care ought to be taken in its identification and attribution.

Racism and anti-semitism are both terms laden with a high degree of emotional content. It is tempting to apply them to a broad range of events, circumstances, and situations that seem to display hatred of Black people on one hand or Jewish people on the other. If they are to be of use in the tasks of diagnosing serious societal maladies, racism and anti-semitism are terms to be used with care and discernment. They risk becoming meaningless when they are applied too quickly or broadly to situations that may warrant a different analysis.

Many Black Americans have yet to learn that the label of racism cannot be pasted on every circumstance we find harmful to us as a group. Likewise, if the term anti-semitism is to retain any currency, it cannot be indiscriminately applied to every situation or circumstance distasteful to Jewish people. A term used to discern attitudes widespread among German and other European citizens about Jews that, in turn, provided a social climate in which the government of the German Third Reich could launch, with minimal opposition, its effort to annihilate European Jewry cannot be used to describe attitudes that lead to conflicts between Jewish merchants and Black customers or Jewish landlords and Black tenants. Nor can the same term be applied to views critical of some policy of the Israeli government. A term that seeks to describe too much ultimately describes nothing of usefulness.

Most especially, anti-semitism is not a term that ought to be applied as a blanket condemnation when a more selective and focused target would be appropriate. "Black anti-semitism" unfortunately has the first quality; it implies there is something endemic in the character, values, or outlooks of almost thirty million Black Americans toward Jewish people when what is at issue are the attitudes and expressions of a miniscule portion of the Black populace.

Getting beyond labels and shibboleths has always been one of the major barriers to communication between different peoples. Anti-semitism is a human virus of such destructive qualities that it is incumbent on every person who values human decency to work for its eradication. Progress toward that end is more likely to occur when consensus is increased and enlarged regarding its nature and where it can appropriately be seen. Black anti-semitism is a label that serves as a barrier to consensus and to authentic discussion with those in Black America who wish to work diligently for the destruction of this oldest of human hatreds.

In the final analysis, racism and anti-semitism are of a single piece. Both are grounded in that strange worldview that requires identifying another group of humans to whom one can point as the pariahs of the earth. There is considerable irony in the fact that the City College of New York whose former chair of its African-American Studies Program is viewed by some as one of the principal exponents of Black anti-semitism should also have a Jewish professor of philosophy on its faculty who has gained notoriety for publishing letters and articles claiming that Black people are less intelligent than whites (*New York Times,* 8 June 1992, A 10). Both men are best seen as tragic examples of the inaneness of which humans are capable and of the price we pay in our society for the right of freedom of expression. Both their viewpoints might also serve as added incentives for Black and Jewish citizens together to address the unfinished agenda of social justice in America.

# Appendix

**SURVEY QUESTIONNAIRE**

**William O. Douglas Institute for the Study of
Contemporary Social Problems**

WE ARE INTERESTED IN YOUR CANDID BELIEFS AND FEEL-ING ON RELIGION AND RELIGIOUS GROUPS. YOUR ANSWERS WILL BE HELD IN STRICTEST CONFIDENCE. FINDINGS WILL BE REPORTED ONLY AS STATISTICAL SUMMARIES; NO RE-PORT WILL EVER BE MADE IN A WAY THAT COULD ALLOW YOUR IDENTIFICATION. *DO NOT WRITE YOUR NAME ON THIS QUESTIONNAIRE.*

MOST OF THE QUESTIONS IN THIS QUESTIONNAIRE ARE FOLLOWED BY A LIST OF POSSIBLE ANSWERS. PLEASE CHOOSE *ONE* ANSWER TO EACH OF THESE QUESTIONS, AND CIRCLE THE *NUMBER* IN FRONT OF THE ANSWER YOU CHOOSE.

**EXAMPLE:**

2. Age

1. under 21        5. 41 to 50
2. 21 to 25        6. 51 to 60
3. 26 to 30        7. over 60
4. 31 to 40

CIRCLING THE "4" WOULD INDICATE THAT YOU ARE IN THE AGE RANGE 31 TO 40. FOR THOSE QUESTIONS REQUIRING A WRITTEN ANSWER, SPACE HAS BEEN PROVIDED.

1. Sex            2. Age

   1. Male          1. under 21
   2. Female        2. 21 to 25
                  3. 26 to 30
                  4. 31 to 40
                  5. 41 to 50
                  6. 51 to 60
                  7. over 60

3. How many years of school did you *complete?*

   1. less than twelve
   2. twelve
   3. one or two years of college
   4. three or more years of college

4. With which of the following racial or ethnic groups do you identify yourself?

   1. White American
   2. Black American
   3. Asian or Pacific American
   4. Native American Indian
   5. Hispanic American (Spanish surname, Latino)

5. What is your yearly income?

   1. $10,000 or less
   2. $11,000–$20,000
   3. $21,000–$30,000
   4. $31,000–$40,000
   5. $41,000–$50,000
   6. over $50,000

6. What is your religious affiliation?

   (a)  Protestant (CONTINUE WITH QUESTION 7)
   (b)  Catholic (SKIP TO QUESTION 8)
   (c)  none (SKIP TO QUESTION 8)

7. If Protestant, what denomination?

   (a)  Methodist AME
   (b)  Methodist AME Zion
   (c)  Methodist CME
   (d)  Baptist
   (e)  Pentecostal/Holiness
   (f)  Other (PLEASE SPECIFY):

8. Which of the following statements comes closest to expressing
   what you believe about God? (CHECK ONLY ONE)

   (a)  I know God exists, and I have no doubts about it.
   (b)  While I have doubts, I feel that I do believe in God.
   (c)  I find myself believing in God some of the time but not
        others.
   (d)  I don't believe in a personal God, but I do believe in a
        higher power of some kind.

(e) I don't know whether there is a God, and I don't believe there is any way to find out.

(f) I don't believe in God.

9. Which of the following statements comes closest to expressing what you believe about Jesus? (CHECK ONLY ONE)

(a) Jesus is the Divine Son of God, and I have no doubts about it.

(b) While I have some doubts, I feel basically that Jesus is divine.

(c) I feel that Jesus was a great man and very holy, but I don't feel him to be the Son of God any more than all of us are children of God.

(d) I think that Jesus was only a man although an extraordinary one.

(e) Frankly, I'm not entirely sure there was such a person as Jesus.

10. The Bible tells of many miracles, some credited to Christ and some to other prophets and apostles. Generally speaking, which of the following statements comes closest to what you believe about Biblical miracles? (CHECK ONE)

(a) I'm not sure whether these miracles really happened or not.

(b) I believe miracles are stories and never really happened.

(c) I believe the miracles happened but can be explained by natural causes.

(d) I believe the miracles actually happened just as the Bible says they did.

(e) I believe some miracles may be explained by natural causes but not all of them.

11. Do you think belief in Jesus Christ as Savior is:

(a) absolutely necessary for salvation,

(b) would probably help, or

(c) probably has no influence?

12. Do you think being a member of your particular religious faith is:

(a) absolutely necessary for salvation,

(b) would probably help, or

(c) probably has no influence?

13. Do you think being completely ignorant of Jesus, as might be the case of people living in other countries, will:

(a) definitely prevent salvation,

(b)  may possibly prevent salvation, or

(c)  probably has no influence on salvation?

14.  How often do you attend Sunday worship services:

(a)  every week

(b)  about two or three times a month

(c)  about once a month

(d)  about once every two or three months

(e)  about once or twice a year

(f)  less than once a year

(g)  never

15.  How often, if at all, are table prayers or grace said before or after meals in your home?

(a)  We say grace at all meals.

(b)  We say grace at least once a day.

(c)  We say grace at least once a week.

(d)  We say grace but only on special occasions.

(e)  We never, or hardly ever, say grace.

16.  How often do you pray privately?

(a)  I never pray or only do so at church services.

(b)  I pray only on very special occasions.

(c)  I pray once in a while but not at regular intervals.

(d)  I pray quite often but not at regular intervals.

(e)  I pray regularly once a week.

(f)  I pray regularly several times a week.

(g)  I pray regularly once a day or more.

17.  How important is prayer in your life?

(a)  extremely important

(b)  fairly important

(c)  not too important

(d)  not important

18.  Following is a series of statements concerning religious attitudes. Please indicate how strongly you agree or disagree with each statement. (CIRCLE THE NUMBER THAT BEST INDICATES WHERE YOU STAND IN RELATION TO THE TWO ENDS OF THE SCALE.)

a.  I believe that there is a physical Hell where people are punished after death for the sins of their lives.

strongly agree  6  5  4  3  2  1  strongly disagree

b. I believe there is a supernatural being, the Devil, who continually tries to lead people into sin.

strongly agree 6 5 4 3 2 1 strongly disagree

c. To me the most important work of the church is saving souls.

strongly agree 6 5 4 3 2 1 strongly disagree

d. I believe there is a life after death.

strongly agree 6 5 4 3 2 1 strongly disagree

e. I believe there is a divine plan and purpose for every living person.

strongly agree 6 5 4 3 2 1 strongly disagree

f. The only benefit one receives from prayer is psychological.

strongly agree 6 5 4 3 2 1 strongly disagree

g. I have a duty to help those who are confused about religion.

strongly agree 6 5 4 3 2 1 strongly disagree

h. Even though it might create some unpleasant situations, it is important to help people become enlightened about religion.

strongly agree 6 5 4 3 2 1 strongly disagree

i. There is no point arguing about religion, because there is little chance of changing other people's minds.

strongly agree 6 5 4 3 2 1 strongly disagree

j. It doesn't really matter what an individual believes about religion as long as he is happy with it.

strongly agree 6 5 4 3 2 1 strongly disagree

k. I believe the world would really be a better place if more people held the views about religion that I hold.

strongly agree 6 5 4 3 2 1 strongly disagree

l. I believe the world's problems are seriously aggravated by the fact that so many people are misguided about religion.

strongly agree 6 5 4 3 2 1 strongly disagree

19. Please indicate how true you believe each of the following statements to be. (CIRCLE THE NUMBER BETWEEN THE

ENDS OF THE SCALE THAT BEST REPRESENTS YOUR VIEWPOINT.)

a. My ideas about religion are one of the most important parts of my philosophy of life.

very true  6  5  4  3  2  1  not at all true

b. I find that my ideas on religion have a considerable influence on my views in other areas.

very true  6  5  4  3  2  1  not at all true

c. Believing as I do about religion is very important to being the kind of person I want to be.

very true  6  5  4  3  2  1  not at all true

d. If my ideas about religion were different, I believe that my way of life would be very different.

very true  6  5  4  3  2  1  not at all true

e. Religion is a subject in which I am not particularly interested.

very true  6  5  4  3  2  1  not at all true

f. I very often think about matters relating to religion.

very true  6  5  4  3  2  1  not at all true

20. For each of the statements that follow, please indicate how strongly you agree or disagree. (CIRCLE THE NUMBER BETWEEN THE ENDS OF THE SCALE THAT BEST REPRESENTS YOUR OWN PERSONAL VIEWPOINT.)

a. Race prejudice is universal. It has always been with us, and it always will be.

Strongly agree  6  5  4  3  2  1  strongly disagree

b. The whites have shown by their actions that they are naturally immoral, vicious, and untrustworthy.

Strongly agree  6  5  4  3  2  1  strongly disagree

c. No matter how nicely they treat a minority person, white people don't really mean it.

Strongly agree  6  5  4  3  2  1  strongly disagree

d. It is usually a mistake to trust a white person.

Strongly agree  6  5  4  3  2  1  strongly disagree

e. Any minority who marries a white is a traitor to his or her people.

Strongly agree  6  5  4  3  2  1  strongly disagree

f. Minority people can expect no real help from white people in the fight against racial discrimination.

Strongly agree  6  5  4  3  2  1  strongly disagree

g. Most white people are always looking for ways to cheat and steal from minority people.

Strongly agree  6  5  4  3  2  1  strongly disagree

h. The Black race has been pushed around long enough; it's about time that the whites were made to get out of the Black community.

Strongly agree  6  5  4  3  2  1  strongly disagree

i. It may be wrong to damn all whites, but it's plain that whites have all the money and power and that they look down on anyone who is Black.

Strongly agree  6  5  4  3  2  1  strongly disagree

j. There are many whites who are not prejudiced and who sincerely believe in racial equality.

Strongly agree  6  5  4  3  2  1  strongly disagree

21. How strongly do you agree or disagree with the following statements? (CIRCLE THE NUMBER BETWEEN THE ENDS OF THE SCALE THAT BEST REPRESENTS YOUR PERSONAL VIEWPOINT.)

a. The Jews must be considered a bad influence on Christian culture and civilization.

Strongly agree  6  5  4  3  2  1  strongly disagree

b. A major fault of the Jews is their conceit, overbearing pride, and their idea that they are the chosen race.

Strongly agree  6  5  4  3  2  1  strongly disagree

c. I think of Jews as being almost Black. They know how it feels to be mistreated.
Strongly agree  6  5  4  3  2  1  strongly disagree

d. One trouble with Jewish businessmen is that they stick together and connive, so that a Gentile doesn't have a fair chance in competition with them.
Strongly agree  6  5  4  3  2  1  strongly disagree

e. Deep down inside, Jews are not as prejudiced as other whites.
Strongly agree  6  5  4  3  2  1  strongly disagree

f. Jews may have moral standards, which they apply in their dealings with others, but with Christians they are unscrupulous, ruthless, and undependable.
Strongly agree  6  5  4  3  2  1  strongly disagree

g. Jews tend to be a parasitic element in society.
Strongly agree  6  5  4  3  2  1  strongly disagree

h. Jews are more willing to combat discrimination.
Strongly agree  6  5  4  3  2  1  strongly disagree

i. The true Christian can never forgive the Jews for their crucifixion of Christ.
Strongly agree  6  5  4  3  2  1  strongly disagree

j. I believe Jews have too much power in the business world.
Strongly agree  6  5  4  3  2  1  strongly disagree

k. Even though the Jews always complain about their persecution throughout history and having been driven from their homeland, the Israelis today are guilty of treating the Palestinians in the same manner.
Strongly agree  6  5  4  3  2  1  strongly disagree

l. Jews are more helpful than harmful in the civil rights struggle.
Strongly agree  6  5  4  3  2  1  strongly disagree

m. On the whole, the Jews have probably contributed less to American life than any other group.
Strongly agree  6  5  4  3  2  1  strongly disagree

n. Jews are more loyal to Israel than America.

Strongly agree  6  5  4  3  2  1  strongly disagree

o. Peace will never come to the Middle East, not because of the Arabs but because of the inflexibility and arrogance of the Israeli.

Strongly agree  6  5  4  3  2  1  strongly disagree

p. Unless Jewish leaders and groups put the anti-Jewish black militants in their place, there will be a lot more anti-Semitism.

Strongly agree  6  5  4  3  2  1  strongly disagree

q. Jews should stop complaining about the Holocaust.

Strongly agree  6  5  4  3  2  1  strongly disagree

r. The Arabs are a bloodthirsty lot who will never rest until they have driven the Jews from Palestine. Therefore, the Israelis have every right to take whatever steps they deem necessary to protect their land.

Strongly agree  6  5  4  3  2  1  strongly disagree

s. Blacks prefer doing business with Jews to non-Jews.

Strongly agree  6  5  4  3  2  1  strongly disagree

22. How often do you have personal contact with Jews?

    1. very often (CONTINUE WITH QUESTION 23)
    2. occasionally (CONTINUE WITH QUESTION 23)
    3. hardly ever (SKIP TO QUESTION 24)
    4. never (SKIP TO QUESTION 24)

23. With whom? (PLEASE CHECK THOSE WITH WHOM YOU HAVE AT LEAST OCCASIONAL CONTACT)

    _____ coworkers
    _____ friends
    _____ teachers
    _____ storekeepers
    _____ employers
    _____ family
    _____ public officials
    _____ public agency representatives
    _____ medical workers
    _____ neighbors
    _____ other businessmen, lawyers

24. Consider each of the following cases individually and indicate whether you approve or disapprove of the decisions.

> CASE A: Although he was strongly recommended by his college teachers, Irving Pindar was rejected by the medical schools to which he applied for admittance. Since other students with poorer college records and less strongly recommended than he were accepted by the same schools to which he applied, it was plain that the reason for Irving's rejection was the fact that he was Jewish.

Do you approve or disapprove of the action taken by the schools with regard to Irving's application for admittance?

Strongly approve 6 5 4 3 2 1 strongly disapprove

> CASE B: Harry Myers and Mary Babcock have been going with one another for six years—ever since they were in college together. Harry is Jewish; Mary is not. Although her friends urge her to break off the relationship, Mary has decided she loves Harry and intends to marry him.

Do you approve of Mary's decision?

Strongly approve 6 5 4 3 2 1 strongly disapprove

> CASE C: Jim Todd was the last member of the squad to vote in the election of captain for next year's football team. It so happened that when it came his turn to vote there was a tie between White and Levine, the two outstanding guards on the team. Jim voted for White. He later explained that he did so because "it just wouldn't be right to have a Jew for football captain."

Do you approve or disapprove of Jim's attitude?

Strongly approve 6 5 4 3 2 1 strongly disapprove

> CASE D: One of the large state universities had a vacancy in its English department. After a careful consideration of the qualifications of all the applicants for the position, the head of the English department and the dean of the college agreed Dr. Harold Bowman was by far the best qualified for the job. An interview with Dr. Bowman confirmed them in their judgment. He was pleasant, attractive in manner, and obviously competent in his field. However when they learned Dr. Bowman was Jewish they decided not to appoint him to the position.

Do you approve or disapprove of the decision made in this case?

Strongly approve 6 5 4 3 2 1 strongly disapprove

25. Finally, using the scale of 1 (highest esteem) to 5 (lowest esteem), please indicate how you rate each of the following leaders of the national Black community (ASSIGN A DIFFERENT NUMBER TO EACH):
*EXAMPLE:* IF YOU HAVE THE VERY HIGHEST RESPECT FOR ANDREW YOUNG, WRITE A "1" IN THE SPACE BEFORE HIS NAME. IF YOUR ESTEEM FOR HIM IS LESS THAN THE VERY HIGHEST WRITE A NUMBER FROM "2" DOWN TO THE VERY LOWEST, A "5." DO THE SAME FOR EACH OF THE OTHER PERSONS ON THE LIST.

_____ Andrew Young

_____ Walter Fauntleroy

_____ Jesse Jackson

_____ Louis Farrakhan

_____ Benjamin Hooks

26. The Catholic Church is too bound up with dogma and superstition to enable it to cope with modern-day problems.

Strongly agree 1 2 3 4 5 6 strongly disagree

27. Catholics have suffered unreasonable religious and social persecution throughout the ages.

Strongly agree 1 2 3 4 5 6 strongly disagree

28. The Catholic belief that theirs is the true church of Christ has led them to feel superior to all other Christians.

Strongly agree 1 2 3 4 5 6 strongly disagree

29. Catholics are a threat to our progressive system with their rigid and outdated opposition to such issues as abortion and divorce.

Strongly agree 1 2 3 4 5 6 strongly disagree

THIS COMPLETES THE SURVEY. THANK YOU VERY MUCH FOR YOUR COOPERATION AND ASSISTANCE.

# Notes

## Introduction

1. Baldwin's essay, entitled "The Harlem Ghetto," originally appeared in the February 1948 issue of *Commentary* and was subsequently reprinted in his well-known collection of essays, *Notes of a Native Son* (Boston: Beacon Press, 1955).

## Chapter 1. The Problem Stated

1. According to Professor Bauer, "the term 'anti-semitism' was coined by individuals in the 1870s who were looking for a pseudoscientific term for 'Jew-hatred', which had come to sound barbaric" (Y. Bauer, *The Holocaust in Historical Perspective,* 1978, p. 8fn.).

2. William J. Wilson, *The Truly Disadvantaged: The Inner City, the Underclass, and Public Policy* (Chicago: University of Chicago Press, 1987) provides a useful analysis of the American underclass, a term that he views as describing approximately the socioeconomic conditions of a discrete segment of the American populace. Regrettably, however, the term has an older and more pejorative history of application almost exclusively to Black Americans (see E. Banfield, *The Unheavenly City: The Nature and Future of Our Urban Crisis* [Boston: Little, Brown, 1968]).

3. The *Brown v. Board of Education* case, which the U.S. Supreme Court decided in 1954, may be viewed as the most dramatic achievement of this alignment of interests, representing as it did the efforts of the N.A.A.C.P. joined by the American Federation of Teachers, the Congress of Industrial Organizations, and nearly every major Jewish organization in the nation (see M. R. Konvitz, *Expanding Liberties: Freedom's Gains in Post-War America* [New York: Viking Press, 1966, p. 255].) The case was a culmination of almost a half century of mutually recognized interests, beginning with the prominent position of Jewish Americans led by Rabbi Stephen S. Wise, in the founding of the N.A.A.C.P. in 1909 (see Benjamin Quarles, *The Negro in the Making of America* [London: Collier-Macmillan, Ltd., 1964], p. 175). Quarles also describes the New Deal's Wagner Labor Relations Act of 1935 and the impetus it gave to the creation of the Committee for Industrial Organization (later the Congress of Industrial Organizations) with its "policy of equality for all workers, black as well as white" as one of the significant outcomes of this period (p. 212). Herbert Garfinkel's analysis of organizational politics in the development of fair employment practices legislation describes a mixed but largely supportive effort by major Jewish organizations, particularly after the Second World War (in *When Negroes March* [New York: Atheneum, 1969]).

4. The Grand Alliance is discussed by a large number of scholars and from a variety of perspectives; see, for example, D. L. Lewis, "Shortcuts to the Mainstream: Afro-American and Jewish Notables in the 1920's and 1930's" in J. R.

Washington, 1984; M. Weitz, "The Shattered Alliance Between U.S. Blacks and Jews" in *Patterns of Prejudice*, 12/3/1978. An extensive bibliography is provided in Davis, "Black-Jewish Alliances", #458–683 (1984), pp. 67–76.

5. See R. Rothenberg, *The Neo-liberals: Creating the New American Politics* (New York: Simon and Schuster, 1984). Rothenberg notes that the editor of *Commentary* was among those who disavowed "their radicalism and would become known . . . as the 'liberal anti-communist'"; still later, they would emerge as the neo-conservatives.

6. This succession pattern has been described extensively in G. Orofsky, *Harlem: The Making of a Ghetto* (New York: Harper and Row, 1963). As Orofsky's analysis makes clear, this process was not primarily one motivated by Jewish beneficence toward Black in-migration but a "response to the same conditions of prosperity that promoted mobility in all the immigrant neighborhoods of Manhattan" (p. 130).

7. Patterns of religious affiliation among Black Americans have shifted slightly but remain basically those described by E. S. Gaustad, "America's Institutions of Faith" (in the first of an annual series of volumes entitled *The Religious Situation* [Boston: Beacon Press, 1968]). Gaustad writes, "The size of the total Baptist family is due in part to the strong attraction that the Baptist tradition has for the American Negro. The last Federal Census of Religion (1936) showed that 67% of all Negro church members were Baptists . . . (while) 3 large Negro bodies (contribute) almost 3 millions more (to the national membership of the ca. 15 million American Methodists") pp. 838–39.

8. In addition to Frazier, see J. R. Washington, *Black Religion* (1966) and B. A. Rosenberg, *The Art of the American Folk Preacher* (New York: Oxford University Press, 1970), chapter 1.

# Chapter 4. Black Protestantism and Anti-Semitism: A Reappraisal

1. These are the elements identified by M. Stohr in his essay "Anti-Semitism as an Ideology" in R. Libowitz, ed., *From Faith to Freedom: A Tribute to Franklin H. Littell* (Oxford: Pergamon Press, 1987), p. 95. Stohr, a West German theologian, is concerned with anti-semitism "against the background of a Christian tradition." However, two additional elements which he discusses have both a religious and a secular dimension: "the degree of marginalization is reduced if Jews lose their identity as Jews in a Christian society, in a socialist, future-oriented society, or in a liberal society through assimiliation or pressure" and Jews as "a foreign minority" question ". . . the absolute claim of Christians to be the only true people of God, or . . . the secularized claim of the majority to be the better race, normal society, or the 'good people.'" For a recent and fuller discussion of the features and characteristics of anti-semitism, see S. Almog, ed., *Anti-semitism through the Ages* (Oxford: Pergamon Press, 1988).

# Bibliographic Appendix

## WARREN LEWIS

As a supplement to Chapter 2 of this volume, which summarizes the principal literature on the topic since the 1940s, this bibliographic appendix annotates a wider sphere of related works that enlarge upon themes discussed in the review of the literature or offer additional observations, findings, or commentaries pertinent to a discussion of the issue of Black anti-semitism. In a few instances, a more detailed discussion of works noted earlier will be found; care has been taken, however, to avoid unnecessary repetition of literature discussed in the main body of the text. For this reason, Chapter 2 and this appendix should be considered as complementary to each other, not as separate treatments of the literature.

This appendix also includes annotations of works, particularly from the decade of the 1960s, that were produced by a small but vocal circle of Black writers who were spokespersons for the new Black Consciousness movement and whose literature fueled much of the debate regarding the putative resurgence of Black anti-semitism. These writings are discussed in this appendix, rather than in Chapter 2, in order to place them in what the author beleives to be their proper context: as significant but not decisive factors in any balanced consideration of the topic.

## Black-Jewish Relations in the South: The Pre–World War I Experience

The attitude of southern Black Americans toward American Jewish citizens was conditioned in a positive way by the Black slave experience and the religious interpretation of that experience. Many references to this dominant aspect of the Black viewpoint on Black-Jewish relations can be found in the literature. The work of two interpreters—Shankman and Evans—examining this theme over the span of almost a century may be taken as representative with a third—Hertzberg—as summarizing this general view.

(See also the special bibliographies in Davis [1964], "Jews as Slave Owners and Slave Traders," # 881–892, p. 90; "Jews in the American Civil War," #893–901, pp. 90–91; "Jews in the Anti-Slavery Movement," # 902, 903, p. 91. See also, Leonard Dinnerstein, ed., *Jews in the South* [Baton Rouge: Louisiana State University Press, 1973], which includes a number of relevant articles, among them, Bertram M. Korn, "Jews and

Negro Slavery in the Old South, 1789–1865." See also: B. W. Korn, *American Jewry and the Civil War* [Philadelphia: Jewish Publication Society of America, 1951]; Philip S. Foner, *The Jews in American History: 1654–1865* [New York: International, 1945], pp. 43–50, 51–62, 63–78; "Jewish-Black Relations in the Opening Years of the Twentieth Century," *Phylon* 36 [December 1975]: pp. 359–367; Hasia R. Diner, *In the Almost Promise Land: Jewish Leaders and Blacks, 1915–1935* [Westport, Conn: Greenwood, 1977]; and M. J. Kohler, *The Jews and the Anti-Slavery Movement* [Baltimore: The Press of the Friedenwald Co., 1896, 25 pp.].

**A.** Arnold Shankman, "Brothers Across the Sea: Afro-Americans on the Persecution of Russian Jews, 1881–1917," *Jewish Social Studies* 37/2 (1975): pp. 114–121. Also "Friend or Foe? Southern Blacks View the Jew, 1880–1935", in Nathan M. Kaganoff and Melvin I. Urofsky, eds., *Turn to the South: Essays on Southern Jewry* (Charlottesville: University of Virginia Press, 1979), pp. 105–23.

Shankman based his study on southern Black newspapers, periodicals, memoirs, and other primary sources. In his 1975 article, Shankman observes that the Black press basically saw "Jew-baiting" in Russia as the equivalent of "Negro-baiting" in the United States. Black Americans denounced Russian Orthodox priests for having "erected an altar in the name of Christianity but with the cardinal principles of Christ left out." Persecutions of Jews in Russia were "sad commentaries on Christianity ... by representatives of Christianity." The Reverend A. J. Carey, Bishop of the A.M.E. Church in Chicago, referring to the rumored "nonsense" that Jews used the blood of a Christian child to make Passover matzohs, sent a telegram to as mass rally in Washington, D.C., on behalf of Russian Jews: "May God aid you in disproving for all time the infamous 'ritual murder' lie" (p. 117).

Shankman quotes the Black American poet, James Weldon Johnson, who stated the prevailing perception of Jews among knowledgeable Black Americans:

> It is the American Negro who can best appreciate the reason for the joy of American Jews, because we are the only other people who have a deep understanding of what the Jews in Russia have suffered. ("Views and Reviews," *New York Age*, 22 March 1917, p. 120)

Precisely because of the benign attitude toward Russian Jewish immigrants, Black Americans were horrified to find Jews who were anti-Black and racist, willing to vote for Jim Crow laws and "just as active in aiding in the persecution of Blacks as any other class of people." One Black editorial indicted a Russian immigrant who, "... but just a few months removed from the massacres of his native country and who came to America to escape prejudice, hatred, and death, was a leader of the recent (1908) Springfield, Illinois, mob. This hardly seems possible" (p. 120).

The general conclusion of Shankman's 1979 essay is that "on the whole blacks viewed Jews more as friends than foes." Unlike other immigrant groups in the South, Jews, as merchants, did not compete with laboring Black workers for jobs, although the Black press sometimes lumped all immigrants together as an economic threat. Black Americans generally came to think of Jewish immigrants as more willing than other newcomers to the South to raise their voices against racism and to treat Black southerners with politeness and courtesy. Black southerners often encountered Jews as dry-goods merchants and as traveling peddlers; Shankman quotes John Dollard (*Caste and Class in a Southern Town* [New Haven: Yale University Press, 1937]) that "whereas whites greeted blacks brusquely with, 'Well, boy, what do you want?' Jews were wont to address Negroes as 'Mr.' or 'Mrs.' and to ask, 'What can I do for you?'" Jewish traders typically put good business ahead of caste principles; they would bargain with Black customers, rather than sticking to a single, fixed-price—a practice that the latter appreciated. Good sense and good business practices worked for good relations between the two groups.

Shankman observes also that, prior to the Civil War, the only Jewish person many Black Americans knew about were those recounted in sermons in the Black churches. Southern Black preaching tended to focus on Old Testament texts, especially those of Moses and the Exodus; both before and after Emancipation, Black preachers would tell their congregations to liken themselves to the children of Israel, first in bondage awaiting freedom; later in freedom to achieve equality. This positive preparation to meet Jewish people in the flesh predisposed Black southerners toward cordial relations with the influx or Russian Jewish immigrants fleeing the pogroms of the 1800s. Shankman concludes: "Almost without exception, Southern blacks welcomed the Jews."

Even "Booker T. Washington, who rarely had a good word for those emigrating from Europe," Shankman notes, "was careful to differentiate Jews from Gentiles." For Washington, to whom advice for Black southerners on how to get ahead was paramount, the stereotype of "Jewish greed" could be viewed as a characteristic worthy of emulation. Jews were persistent, thrifty, economically shrewd, lived simply, enjoyed family solidarity, invested their profits in their education of their children, would do almost anything to satisfy a customer, did not mind living in nonwhite neighborhoods, would allow Black customers to try on clothing for size (which white haberdashers would not), and provided jobs for Black southerners.

**B.** Steven Hertzberg, *Strangers within the Gate City: The Jews of Atlanta,, 1845–1915* (Philadelphia: Jewish Publication Society of America, 1978), pp. 195–99.

Hertzberg examines the Black press of the Old South for attitudes toward Jewish immigration in the pre–World War I period. The *Voice of the Negro* was found to be one of the most blatant on the issue, with cartoons opposing the flood tide of immigrants who would be competing for jobs with Black southerners and equating "nihilist," "socialist," "anarchist," and "Jew." In an editorial (September 1905) the paper warned:

> The men who are plotting this immigration scheme do not stop to think how, in filling the South with cheap labor from Europe, they would thrust wages down lower and lower; how the Negroes and low laborers of Europe would clash at every point, and how the very integrity of the pure white south would be threatened by intermingling with this semi-white class of people. These immigrants would be a serious factor in any national crisis. Aliens always are.

The editor of the *Voice* could not see why whites would want to replace the "sunniest-dispositioned, most patient, most law-abiding, the meekest and the best working people in the world" with "the scum of Europe." Similarly the *Atlanta Independent* warned the ruling class that:

> These foreigners will put the devil in the Negroes' heads and another menace will be added to our labor and race problem. . . . The white man will (then) be perfectly willing to exchange his overpaid anarchist laborer for his old, under-paid and half-fed Negro service [*sic*]. (*Atlanta Independent*, 23 March 1907, p. 4; 19 June 1909, p. 4)

Hertzberg concludes that the reference to "semi-white" European scum meant, in this specific context Italians; but as Jews were also perceived as not quite white, they were included. This native racism he sees as purely economic in motive and not related to religious prejudice (p. 196).

(David Hellwig's study, *The Afro-American and the Immigrant, 1880–1930* [Syracuse University, unpublished doctoral dissertation, 1973] accords with this general view. Ex-slaves were idealistically committed to a sympathetic response to the poor, oppressed, and persecuted immigrants, at least in the nineteenth century. The farther away Black Americans moved from slavery, however, and the more they became socialized in the ways of the American mainstream, the less sympathetic they were to incoming competitors.)

Hertzberg also notes the number of emulation motifs, rooted in the African-Israeli theme of Black religion (p. 193). Black identification with the children of Israel in Egyptian slavery and suffering, the wilderness wandering and pilgrimage toward freedom, led to recommendation of perceived traits of modern Jews, as well: family solidarity, hard work and clever business dealings, high esteem for education, perseverance in the common struggle toward civil rights, ethnic separatism, and mutual support. These positive stereotypes, however, could become negative when group solidarity was perceived as clannishness that excluded non-Jews, when education became elitism, and when hard work and economic acumen became "Jewish greed." Thus, the recommendation of some Black leaders to "imitate the Jews" was offered with a degree of ambiguity, and the ambiguity turned to disillusion when some Jews were seen as not living up to Black expectations. In particular, when some Jews were not faithful to civil right ideals, Black Americans would charge that Jewish people, who had suffered so much and who should have learned their lessons on social ethics from Moses and the prophets, "ought to know better."

**C.** Eli N. Evans, *The Provincials: A Personal History of Jews in the South* (New York: Atheneum, 1973), especially pp. 291–326, "Jews and Blacks."

Evans similarly deals with the close attachment that the southern Black church historically has had for Biblical Judaism. Whereas white Protestantism turned the Old Testament into a prophecy of the New— a precursor of resurrection and retribution—Black Protestantism took Old Testament stories and heroes as they found them. Black preachers sang their sermons about Moses leading the children of Israel out of bondage, of Joshua and the battle of Jericho, and of Daniel in the den of lions and made them come alive not only as signposts to the New Covenant but as heroes of the Old, to be imitated in patience while in bondage and in bravery while striving for freedom (pp. 296–97). As an untold number of Black songs depicted, Black southerners identified their own plight with that of the Israelites in Egyptian bondage and with the followers of Moses and Joshua en route to the Promised Land.

Evans recounts:

A Black preacher in Mississippi told me his favorite stories from the Old Testament: "Well, there's Joshua . . . we sing about him, you know."
  "Yes sir," I said. "and what's the lesson?"
  "If you keep circling and making enough noise the walls will come a'tumbling down," he answered. "And then there's Daniel—he would not bow down and the lions stood there looking at him because of his faith. And of course there's Moses—leading the children of Israel out of slavery into the promised land—that was Dr. King's favorite.

"To many Blacks," Evans concludes, "George Wallace and 'Bull' Connor were the Pharaohs: Selma and Montgomery, the land of Egypt; and Martin Luther King, their Moses."

This special identification with ancient Israel in the religious consciousness of Black Protestants is noted also by Peter I. Rose, *Mainstream and Margins: Jews, Blacks, and Other Americans* (New Brunswick, N.J.: Transaction, 1983), pp. 147–64:

That so much (in Negro spirituals and Negro worldview, including the Jews) is derived from the fifth book of the Pentateuch is not to say that Blacks have been unaware of the portrayal [sic] of Jews in the New Testament, nor that as listeners to evangelical circuit riders or radio crusaders they could have avoided hearing about 'the perfidious Jews,' 'the Christ-killers.' Still, Blacks know that like Moses, Jesus was a Jew, and most have difficulty reconciling the wholesale dismissal of his parentage because of the acts of a small group of betrayers. While it has been argued that 'if blacks are anti-Semitic, it is because they are Christian,' most evidence belies such a claim. One must look elsewhere for roots of whatever Black anti-Semitism exist. (p. 149)

Evans is aware of the literature regarding Jewish slaveholding, citing the study by Korn (op. cit.) who asserts that southern Jews, for the most part, shared the racial mentality of their white neighbors:

There is not recorded a single abolitionist among the Jews of the South. . . . Jews participated in every aspect and process of exploitation . . . testifying against Negroes in court, apprehending a runaway slave, inflicting punishment upon a convicted Negro. . . . Jewish owners of slaves were not exceptional figures. (p. 299–300)

(See also Sherman Labovitz, *Attitudes toward Blacks Among Jews* [San Francisco: R and E Research Associates, 1975; based on Labovitz's *Attitudes towards Blacks among Jews: Historical Antecedents and Current Concerns*, University of Pennsylvania, unpublished doctoral dissertation, 1972]. Labovitz asserts that "Jews as a body took no action either pro or con in relation to slavery. . . . There were the significant few who actively advocated social justice and equality while the majority made peace with a system that systematically emasculated and dehumanized Blacks. Jewish attitudes were very much akin to those Gentiles with whom they lived and worked" [1975, pp. 10, 12].)

Nevertheless, Evans argues that Black and Jewish southerners maintained a special relationship, which first grew out of their commercial contacts and was strengthened by a mutual fear of the society in which they lived. Slaves and freedpersons could tell that the Jewish people with strange accents and different ways were different from other whites. The Jewish southerners were not large slave owners nor farmers; they were more salespersons in attitude, grateful to customers of whatever color.

All these factors, says Evans, led to "marked differences between the attitudes of Northern and Southern blacks towards Jews . . . Southern blacks don't look on Jews as 'whites' but as a sympathetic third race, in contrast to the other whites they encounter" (p. 305). "A black civil rights leader confessed, Evans recalls, "that he always carefully used the phrase 'Jewish community' because in the small town he grew up in, 'the way the white Southerner said "Jews" always sounded like "nigger" to me'" (p. 306).

This legacy of tolerable relations has bequeathed some new, equally positive images and some irony. Evans observes that to Mississippi Negroes during the civil rights struggles of the 1950s and 1960s, the term "Jew federal lawyer" came to mean a sympathetic, hardheaded person with the tools to help when trouble started. On the other hand, an old German Jewish merchant and fourth generation Mississippian commented on the death of the three civil rights workers in Philadelphia, Mississippi: "Sure I felt sorry for those boys. But nobody asked them to come down here and meddle with our way of life" (pp. 324, 326)

For the literature that challenges this essentially positive view of Black-Jewish relations in the pre–World War I South, see W. J. Moses (*The

*Golden Age of Black Nationalism, 1850–1925* [Hamden, Conn.: Archon/ Shoe String, 1978], p. 98), who interprets Booker T. Washington's "Atlanta Compromise" speech as having . . . "played upon the Anglo-Americans' xenophobic fears of Catholics and Jews, of southern Europeans and Slavs, 'those of foreign birth and strange tongue and habits.' He conjured up images of dirty-bearded and foul-breathed anarchy streaming into the cities of the North. . . ." See also Hortense Powdermaker, *Stranger and Friend* (New York, 1966); Richard Wright, *Black Boy: A Record of Childhood and Youth* (New York: Harper, 1937) pp. 53–54; Horace Mann Bond, "Negro Attitudes Toward Jews," in Jewish *Social Studies* 27, no. 1 (January 1965): pp. 3–9.

The Wright-Bond citations are frequently quoted as canonical examples of Black anti-semitism. While they are too extensive to quote in this essay, it is of interest to note that both Wright and Bond recount experiences when they were quite young—Wright when he was about eight years old and Bond when he was twelve. Ironically, both recite their childhood experiences of anti-semitism in order to indicate their subsequent understanding of its negative qualities. Bond, in particular, notes:

> It is my considered view that Negro attitudes and actions towards Jews that are frequently interpreted as "anti-semitic" actually lack the sinister thought-content they are sometimes advertised as holding. The occasional riots against small businessmen and landlords in Harlem—persons who may happen to be Jews—do not, in my opinion, actually possess the "classic" emotional load of aggression against a Jewish "race" or "religion" that has been considered the essence of "anti-semitism" (p. 7)
>
> If religion and emotions engendered by religious teachings are indeed a basic key, we need to note that the religion of the Negro slave early identified the group with the history of the Jewish people. Perhaps this feeling of identification is disappearing, but as a small child, I remember singing, not often in *our* church, because we used the Congregational Puritan hymnal but at least in Sunday School and always in school—even in a Congregational church school—such songs as "Go Down Moses" . . . "Little David" and "Joshua Fit the Battle of Jericho". . . . I would defy anyone who said that there was any idea of anti-semitism among the simple people I saw. (p. 9)

## Black-Jewish Relations: The World War II Era

**A.** Lunabelle Wedlock, *The Reaction of Negro Publications and Organizations to German Anti-Semitism,* The Howard University Studies in the Social Sciences, III/2 (Washington, D.C.: Howard University, 1942).

The work of this unsung scholar, further enhanced with a foreword by Ralph Bunche (pp. 7–10), was completed during wartime and before the refinement of statistical studies on Black-Jewish relations in the social sciences. It opens a window on the mind of Black America in the early 1940s more adequately and objectively than any other work.

Bunche's foreword, itself worthy of note, summarizes a perspective on Black American attitudes toward Jewish people as inclusive and insightful as anything written in the past half century. For Bunche, Jewish people were both as loveable and unlovable as Gentiles in equivalent circumstances. Bunche expresses his regret over the existence of Black anti-semitism; at the same time, he understands it to be, in part, borrowed from the racism of the surrounding society; in part, scapegoating; in part, the predictable resentment bred of unpleasant economic contacts. Evenhandedly, Bunche has no pity for stereotyping within either group:

> Many Jews exhibit the same prejudiced, stereotyped attitudes towards Negroes that are characteristic of so many members of the dominant Gentile population. Likewise, many Negroes embrace enthusiastically the anti-Jewish concepts which have attained wide currency, and adapt them to their own devices. Clearly, Jewish Negrophobism and Negro anti-Semitism are ridiculous examples of "the pot calling the kettle black." (p. 7)

Wedlock studied the attitudes of Black Americans toward German anti-semitism and toward American Jews as reflected in the Black press. She supplemented her study with numerous interviews, a cogent historical perspective on the history of anti-semitism, a careful analysis of the social position of Jews and Black Americans, and a discussion of the racist fallacies implicit in allegations about "Jewish traits" and comparisons of the Jewish plight in Germany and the plight of Black Americans. She attempted to summarize the attitude of Black Americans nationally but controlled her study for regional differences, with a sensitive regard for the religious factor in this issue.

Aware that some Black Americans were thoroughly racist in their attitude toward Jewish people, Wedlock's thesis considers Black anti-semitism "as an outgrowth of the economic relationships existing between the two groups because they have to a large extent originated out of a real or imagined exploitation" (p.14). Citing the familiar examples of exploitation—from the Bronx Slave Market to the Bronzeville war of the bourgeois capitalists—Wedlock amplifies her version of the economic anti-semitism "contact" theory, seeing all other impulses toward anti-semitism as tributary (pp. 26–30, 116–18). Whether appropriation of Nazi propaganda or Christian charitable sympathy for those similarly persecuted, Black attitudes toward Jewish people seem always to be elaborated in some way—whether among the poor or among the rising middle class—in relation to the economic theme. She observed that hostilities between the two communities declined when Jewish store owners in Chicago responded to Black demands and hired staff across racial lines but that Black upward mobility subsequently presented a new form of the problem when competition emerged between both groups in the owner class and at the management level (pp. 170–71).

Following the familiar themes of paralleling Black and Jewish experiences and of encouraging Black Americans to emulate the Jews, Wedlock reports that some editorialists saw encouragement for Black Americans in the endurance of the Jewish people under persecution. The God of righteousness and the moral sense of the world would not forever tolerate such injustices. Besides, in an aside to the German theory of racial superiority, she notes that "Africans were building pyramids and Jews temples three thousand years ago, while Germans were still barbarians" (p. 35). German anti-semitism was seen as a theological failure in abandoning the God of the Jews and reverting to an old pagan cult (p. 36). Black Americans, contrariwise, when brought to America as slaves, had found solace in the Old Testament, "the Jewish soul turned wrong side out." Yet, just as German Christians persecuted Jews, so white Christians in America persecuted Black Christians, so that the Black identification with the rejected Jews was on-going (p. 49; see also pp.51–52).

Wedlock discusses the anti-semitism of Sufi Abdul Hamid, Harlem's "Black Hitler" (pp. 72–73, 132) and that of one of Chicago's Black newspapers, *Dynamite*. Wedlock interviewed the latter's editor, H. George Davenport (pp. 167–77), who advocated that the effect of Hitlerism might be pro-Negro by eliminating "Jewish greed" and reports the denunciation of this stance by noted Black Americans, such as Adam Clayton Powell and Lawrence Reddick. (For studies of Hamid and Davenport, see Roi Ottley, below.)

Where Wedlock considers the religious factor, she finds it to be either a countervailing influence to anti-semitism or an ambiguous contributory influence at the disposal of economic anti-semitism. She finds moral exhortations in Catholic periodicals against anti-Jewish racism in Germany and anti-Negro racism in America (pp. 59–60, 153). (She comments cryptically of the Roman Catholic press: "An organ of the Catholic Church, one of the most vigorous critics of the Jews in the Middle Ages, now has come out in their defense" [p. 136]).

She reports on a Baptist press survey of the persecution of the Jews in many countries as optimistic that "well-nigh universal protest" against such persecution would become so organized that "enraged public sentiment" would benefit other persecuted groups: "In other words, persecution of the underlings of society is about to be outlawed." *The Sunday School Informer* (Tennessee) went on to say that the bad Jewish habit of racial separatism—a Jewish trait which Jesus had deplored—had made Jews unwelcome in the nations of "a vile and unsocial world." Therefore, concluded the Baptist editorial, "We should follow the example of Jesus and aid them" (pp. 60–61). In a more anti-semitic vein, the Baptist Sunday School Journal interpreted the antiquity of anti-semitism in terms of a "peculiar Jewish philosophy of life" that included "a racial superiority complex at its base" and an "authoritarian attitude of tyranny toward undesirable minority groups." Jewish business practices, said to cause no "native revolt of conscience" in its practitioners, are seen as rooted in their Biblical ancestors. Cheating was habitual among the patriarches, as was usury, a "racial trait which is traceable even back to Rebecca, the mother of Israel." American Christians, concludes the editor, ought to ignore the chicanery, superiority complex, and other many faults of the Jews and extend aid to them in their time of need ("Anti-Semitism in our World and Its Basic Causes," April 1935, pp. 6–9). In a similar editorial, ("Anti-Semitism on the Increase," April 1938, pp. 3–4), the writer laments that America is in no position to protest the international financial power of the "seed of Abraham," lest they close the financial arteries of our commercial system." The editorial concludes amiably: "Even though Jews rejected Christ let not Christians reject them, but receive them into their sympathies and hearts in the spirit and name of Jesus."

In the pages of her media sources, Wedlock found no agitation about "Christ-killers" among conservative Black Protestants, although she did find occasional willingness to use the unretouched Biblical image of crafty Hebrews, pockets filled with Egyptian gold and silver, as a way of expressing economic anti-semitism. She found that the Black press in the South both was more religious in tone in its discussion of anti-semitism and attacked the Jews on economic grounds less frequently than the northern Black press, although southern Black editors faithfully reported harsh news of Jewish-Black relations in the North. "There is less anti-Semitism among Negroes in the South, because of the smaller percentage of Jews there, and because of the fact that there are "few contacts between the two groups" (pp. 185–86).

Wedlock is critical of much of the Black press; she particularly singles out *The Voice of Ethiopia* and the Roman Catholic publication, *The African* (pp. 61–62, 136) for their "narrowly chauvinistic . . . extremely limited" Black-oriented "extremely "race-conscious" perspective (p. 193). This reified worldview predicated not on religion but race, when taken together with a "consideration of the economic position and activities of the Jew, which is based on false ideas," though it "sometimes exists without hatred for the racial group," more often "engenders anti-Semitism which may or may not become crystallized" (p. 191). Wedlock found no widespread, organized Black anti-semitism, tending rather to see "some of the Anti-Semitism among Negroes" as their "absorption of the accepted philosophy" of racial theories that had come to be "widely accepted for almost a century" (p. 207).

Prophetic of the time when ideological Black militancy would organize these, as yet disparate elements into a social propaganda explicitly based on religion and race, Wedlock comments toward the close of her study:

> In recent years, there has been an attempt by some Negro leaders to make Negroes conscious of their African heritage and of a bond with other colored groups the world over. Despite this trend toward a glorification of race and color, the fostering of an extreme race-consciousness has met with little success among the mases the masses of Negroes." (p. 203)

**B.** Anti-semitism in America in the 1930s and 1940s was aggravated initially by disagreement over American foreign policy, by pro-German propagandizing, and by antipathy toward communists. Wherever residual white Christian anti-semitism was available to be pressed into service under racism, both Catholic and Protestant demagogues made use of it. Within the Black community, however, the efficient cause of anti-Jewish sentiments remained that of economic contact that became almost exclusively the focus of Black commentaries during this period.

Where religion was a factor at all, it tended to work against Black racism and prejudice and for better Black-Jewish relations. But rural sharecroppers, innocent before the impersonal demands of bourgeois capitalism, once they had migrated to the color-coded ghettos of the North, turned to spiteful envy of the success of Jewish entrepreneurs. Benign Black preconceptions about the modern-day children of Israel bred of their respect for the Chosen People of the Bible and the Old Testament heroes, the Christian love ethic, and the southern experience of peaceful relations with southern Jews were no match for the harsh realities of ghetto life, in which "the Jew," far from being a persecuted minority suffering under similar circumstances, came to be seen as the economic master.

Some positive influences in the North mitigated against this summary classification of Jews by Black Americans. Many Jews in the northern ghettos were, in fact, conscientious businesspeople, as their southern counterparts had been, and treated Black Americans decently. A wealthy, vocal, and politically aggressive minority of Jewish leaders, particularly those who helped establish and fund the Black-Jewish alliance, were keenly committed to civil rights for all Americans and especially for persecuted minorities, Black and Jewish alike. Labovitz (1975, pp. 8–33), documents this history and quotes at least one Black editorialist, Chandler Owen, who asked: "Should the Negro Hate the Jew?" (*Chicago Defender*, 8 November 1941) as answering:

> When Negroes fail to get jobs, they often ascribe their failure to Jewish employers or stockholders even though in many cases Jews have no connection whatever with the stores or factories concerned.

This positive statement, however, is overbalanced by a handful of statements from Black spokespersons whose comments also came to be nearly canonical in the debate that followed and are to be encountered in quotation or by allusion everywhere in the literature on both sides of the issue. Perhaps an analogy best depicts the overall situation in the era before Black militancy emerged to unify the several elements into an ideological whole. Just as the early Christians expressed anti-Jewish sentiments in their social-theological disagreement with normative Judaism, it may be urged that they were not anti-semites in the sense of mystical race-hatred that began to characterize Catholic Europe after Constantine, that became the "black plague" of European Christendom in

the Middle Ages, and that eventuated in the twentieth-century Holocaust. So also with Black Americans. Anti-Jewish sentiments expressed
during and immediately after World War II, though aggravated in part
by European-style anti-semitism in the harangues of ghetto anti-semites
during the war, were neither traditional race-hatred nor mystical, reli-
gious-motivated and anti-semitism. They reflect, instead, an anti-Jewishness born of economic frustration and intensified by the social
characteristics of the Jewish community, which were dramatically different from those of the Black community: separatism, "clannishness," and
elitism reinforced by a religious identity and worldview partly familiar
to Black Americans (in that it derived in large measure from the Old
Testament) but partly alien (in that it was European Judaism unmelted
in the American social amalgam.)

For further discussion on Black-Jewish relations in this period, see
Howard W. Odum, *Race and Rumors of Race* (Chapel Hill: University of
North Carolina, 1943), especially pp. 132–35, "When Hitler Takes
Over." Odum relates the widespread folk myths in the Black community
during the war that the Nazis would put Black people in charge of
America and that the Negro's "day" would come, when Hitler won the
war (e.g., "When Mr. Hitler gets over here, we will sit in the front of the
bus," folks said to one another; and a housemaid is alleged to have said
to her mistress, "when Mr. Hitler gets over here, you'll be doing my
work."). According to Odum, Black Americans apparently did lend an
ear to Axis propaganda, and some funds were rumored to have been
channeled to the United States to foment an uprising. One rumor, which
many American Jews believed, held that "The Negroes are all organized
through the churches. They have received and are still receiving Nazi
propaganda. They can arise and attack the whites whenever they want."
Utterly unaware of Nazi racism or German attitudes toward dark-
skinned people in general but sadly indicative of Black social conditions
of the era, one sentiment reputedly popular in Black communities ran:

> My country's tired of me,
> I'm going to Germany,
> Where I belong.

In none of this, however, does Odum report any religious anti-semit-
ism. See also: Roi Ottley and William J. Weatherby, *The Negro in New
York: An Informal Social History* (Dobbs Ferry, N.Y.: Oceana, 1967) in
which the authors state that there was no organized anti-semitism in
Harlem but that propaganda articulated resentment against a very real
economic foe by projecting animosity on an imaginary foe, the mythic
"Jew" of Nazi-hatred. See especially the lengthy bibliography on "Black
Americans Support of Jews Against Hitler and Nazism" in Davis (1984,
#208–351, pp. 48–56); and James S. Stemons, *As Victim to Victims: An
American Negro Laments with Jews* (New York: Fortuny's, 1941) for a classic
statement of the "we suffer alike" theme.

See also Steven Bloom, *Interactions between Blacks and Jews in New York City, 1900–1930, as Reflected in the Black Press* (New York University, unpublished doctoral dissertation, 1973). This study of a slightly earlier period concludes that no fundamental antipathy toward Jews existed among Black Americans and that the Black press tended more to generalize about the friendliness of Jews than about their hostility toward Black Americans. The study notes that such Black publications as *New York Age, New York Amsterdam News, Crisis, Messenger, Negro World,* and *The Chicago Defender* consistently opposed white anti-semitism and typically saw a parallel between the European mistreatment of Jews and the circumstances of Black Americans. In contrast, Isabel Bioko Price, *Black Response to Anti-Semitism: Negroes and Jews in New York, 1880 to World War II* (University of New Mexico, unpublished doctoral dissertation, 1973), argues that the Harlem riot of 1943 demonstrated the superficiality of the Black-Jewish alliance and that five hundred smashed plate-glass windows on 125th Street made clear, at least, the degree of Black economic anti-semitism. Jews, as whites, were seen to be passing Black Americans on the social-economic ladder, leaving the latter deprived and ignored.

See also: William Muraskin, "Black Anti-Semitism in the 1930's," *Community Issues* (February 1972): p. 9; Harold Orlansky, "A Note on Anti-Semitism among Negroes," *Politics 2* (August 1945): pp. 250–252; Chandler Owen, "Negro Anti-Semitism: Cause and Cure," *National Jewish Monthly* 57, no. 1 (September 1942): pp. 14–15; Ben Richardson, "Anti-Semitism and the Negro," *The Protestant* 5, no. 9 (June 1944); Ben Richardson, "No Anti-Semitism (By Negroes): This is Our Common Destiny," *People's Voice* (7 August 1943), p. 21; David Levering Lewis, "Shortcuts to the Mainstream: Afro-American and Jewish Notables in the 1920's and 1930's," in Joseph R. Washington, Jr., *Jews in Black Perspectives: A Dialogue* (Madison, N.J.: Fairleigh Dickinson University Press, 1984, pp. 89–97).

**C.** Roi Ottley, *"New World a-Coming: Inside Black America"* (Boston: Houghton Mifflin, 1943). Ottley's work is one of the most important commentaries on the period under examination. He notes Marcus Garvey and other "race missionaries" and "race apostles" who served to keep expressions of Black Nationalism alive and thereby stimulate concomitant expressions of anti-semitism (p. 104). Positive expressions of racism in favor of one group or color necessarily implies, in Ottley's view, a depreciation of other colors and usually stimulates hostility toward other groups. Ottley describes Harlem's "jobs-for-Negroes" campaign and Sufi Abdul Hamid (formerly Eugene Brown of Philadelphia) with his press agent, Ace Parker, as little more than a race-oriented protection racket. With slogans of "Share the Jobs!", these anti-semites waged a propaganda war against any white merchant in principle, but focused parimarily on the majority who were Jewish, ignoring Greek, Italian, and Irish businesses.

When the huge statuesque figure of Sufi, with his brown bearded face and searching eyes, resplendently dressed in turban, green velvet blouse, Sam Brown belt, riding habit, patent leather boots, and wearing a black crimson-lined cape carelessly around his shoulders, strode out on Lenox Avenue . . . [and] established the Negro Industrial Clerical Alliance, . . . as Harlem would say—the panic was on!

Sufi was quickly branded "Black Hitler" or "Harlem Hitler" and his chief lieutenant, Francis Minor, "a vivid, intense young man" was labeled a "Goering," sobriquets that neither dramatically inclined figure found disagreeable. Eyewitnesses said they had seen Nazi agents make direct contact with Sufi. Sufi, subsequently charged with fomenting racial strife between Negroes and Jews on account of the many anti-semitic handbills he and his followers distributed, endured a three-day trial but was acquitted (pp. 116–21). (See also Claude McKay, "Harlem Runs Wild," *Nation* 140/3639, 3 April 1935, pp. 382–383.)

In his chapter on "Jews in Negro Life" (pp. 122–36), Ottley argues that Black anti-semitism, while "complex and curious," was essentially an "artificial issue" and of recent manifestation, "perhaps about ten years old." It grew up out of Marcus Garvey's complaint about "Jewish control of the Negro's economic life." Although Garvey disclaimed being an anti-semite, the times intensified the impression: Nazi propaganda was rife, American isolationism and pro-German feelings were rampant, Black Americans were afraid of losing their jobs to a trickle of Jewish immigrants fleeing Nazi Germany who, though few in number, were numerous in rumor. Ottley summarizes:

Actually, the whole business of anti-Jewish sentiment among Negroes is largely an urban manifestation, and stems directly from the Negro's own depressed condition socially and economically, and is essentially an *anti-white* manifestation. . . . Back in the last century, when Negroes were in daily competition with the Irish, conflicts arose between them. Most of the early race riots in New York City involved the Negroes and the Irish. (p. 123)

Just as Black Americans had absorbed English and "blue-blood" anti-Irish prejudice in their economic struggle with the waves of Irish immigrants, so now they were in an economic stand-off with "the Jew" whom they came to know primarily through usurious credit scams, working for Jewish housewives in the Bronx Slave Market, and dealing with small merchants, landlords, rent collectors and agents, and pawnbrokers in the ghetto. Two Black newspaper reporters, Ella Baker and Marvel Cooke, investigated this situation and found that Jewish employers frequently underpaid, overworked, rigidly supervised, and did not feed their Black employees well; frequently also, the latter had to haggle for their wages when their day's work was over. One result of this investigative journalism was the formation of a semi-official group known as the Committee on Street-Corner Markets; another was the creation of a public inquiry. Not surprisingly, the inquiry found that free labor markets had existed in every large city (with or without Jewish populations) since as early as 1834, attended by similarly uncontrolled economic exploitation. Public investigation did lead, however, to limited reform of the Bronx Slave Market and some rectification in economic relations was achieved.

Ottley concludes:

> Being of very recent vintage, anti-Semitism has hardly penetrated the surface of the Negro's thinking, and thus has little or no roots. . . .

He quotes Lawrence D. Reddick ("Anti-Semitism among Negroes," *Negro Quarterly* 1, no. 2 [Summer 1942]: pp. 112–122) who notes the "small body of rhymes in (Black) folklore that stem from the anti-Jewish elements in the Christian tradition" and notes:

> If these have been translated into active opinions, it certainly is not apparent in Negro life, he [Reddick] says. Negroes have never been associated with any overt forms of anti-Semitism. . . . (p. 128)

Thus, through the first half of the twentieth century, knowledgeable observers, both Black and Jewish, were inclined to speak of or describe generally benign relationships between Black and Jewish Americans, strained—when tensions appeared—primarily by the nature of economic contacts chiefly between Black residents and Jewish merchants, landlords, and other business people in northern cities.

## African-American Ideological Anti-Semitism: Black Militancy

Organized expressions of anti-semitism that are found since World War II can be located chiefly in three settings: in the Nation of Islam (more popularly referred to as the Black Muslims), in a small circle of writers and intellectuals, and among a smaller group of popular public figures whose limited influence, in the main, peaked in the early 1970s and who no longer enjoy an organizational base.

For the Nation of Islam, as for Stokely Carmichael, Eldridge Cleaver, H. Rap Brown, spokespersons for the Student Non-Violent Coordinating Committee, for the 1968 National Conference on Black Power; and for Huey Newton and Bobby Seale of the Black Panther Party, agreement with the now-rescinded United Nations resolution, which equated Zionism with racism, made possible a whole new range of anti-Israeli, anti-Zionist, and anti-semitic rhetoric. The Black Panther Party and SNCC no longer exist; the Nation of Islam continues to thrive as a more viable form of Black religious sectarianism that combines both a strong social message with a distinctive anti-semitic philosophy.

(C. Eric Lincoln, *The Black Muslims in America* [Boston: Beacon, 1961] is still, after thirty years, the basic study of the Nation of Islam; see also Horace Mann Bond, "Negro Attitudes Towards Jews" [*op. cit.*]. For studies of Black militancy and anti-semitism, see Marvin Weitz, "The Shattered Alliance Between U.S. Blacks and Jews," [*Patterns of Prejudice* 12, no. 3, 1978]; Henry Cohen, *Justice, Justice: A Jewish View of the Black Revolution* [New York: Union of American Hebrew Congregations, 1969], Nathan C. Belth, *A Promise to Keep: A Narrative of the American Encounter with Anti-Semitism* [New York: *New York Times*/ADL of B'nai B'rith, 1979]). Belth concludes that the Black Power/Black Nationalist movements, beginning with the Black Muslims, represented "as much a rejection of the established Negro leadership as a revolt against the white-dominated society. Separatism and rejection of Jewish leadership in civil rights activities went along with a turning away from 'the Christian ethic so central in American Negro life.'")

The work of militant Black poets, essayists, and other writers are represented by LeRoi Jones ("Black Art" in Jones and Larry Neal, *Black Fire, An Anthology of Afro-American Writing* [New York, 1966] and Larry Neal, "White Liberals vs. Black Community," *Liberator* 6–7, [July 1966]).

Jones/Baraka is a persuasive poet who lodges a familiar complaint against the cultural imperialism of European-American society and what he terms the "patronizing condescension" of Jewish and other white liberals. His poetry is a reification of Negritude, an emotional canonization of "Black" as the objective consideration for all cultural connotations, whether racially specific or not. In *Raise Rays Raze: Essays Since 1965* (New York: Random House, 1969; Vintage, 1972), Jones/Baraka expands his racial rage not only against Jews but everyone, including "redfaced Irishmen and swarthy Italians" as well as (Black) stooges who symbolize a white system of laws that breaks the back of Black people in Jones/Baraka's hometown of Newark.

See also Maulana Ron Karenga, *The Quotable Karenga* [Los Angeles, 1967]; Allon Schoener, ed., *Harlem on My Mind* [New York: Random House, 1968]; interview with Julius Lester in Nat Hentoff, "Jews and Negroes," *Evergreen Review* [April 1969]. Lester, a radio personality in New York, who was at the center of Black anti-semitism controversies in that city in the late 1960s, later wrote his "Confessions of a Former Anti-Semite" [The *Village Voice,* 10 September 1979] in which he stated:

> I am deeply sorry that black leadership spoke as it did, because my humanity as a black person was diminished. The differences and tensions between Blacks and Jews are real, but the positions espoused recently by black leaders were not 'our Declaration of Independence,' as Kenneth Clark put it. They merely showed that blacks, too, can be Germans.

One of the more interesting publications from this circle appeared in the Winter 1977 issue of *Black Books Bulletin* (5/4, "Blacks and Jews," Chicago: Institute of Positive Education). Edited by Haki R. Madhubuti, it contains a number of brief articles that purport to represent historical, etymological, and sociopolitical analyses of the Black-Jewish experience. Doris Darkwah, for example, is author of an article titled "The Role of Africa in the Rise of Judaism," which attempts to replace the Biblical account of Jewish origins with a Black-African version of the African origins of Judaism; it represents a fascinating hypothesis that is riddled with factual error (e.g., "the Old Testament itself was put together by Greeks . . .", p. 70). John H. Clark ("Some Scratches on a Time Bomb—Israel and South Africa: The Unholy Alliance Against African People") provides a strident indictment of Israel's diplomatic recognition of South Africa, while William H. Pritchard ("Blacks, Jews, and Negro Zionists: A Crisis in Negro Leadership") argues that "quisling Negro Zionist leaders" are in the pockets of American Zionist Jews.

(See also Larry Neal, editor of the *Liberator*, whose article "Black Power in the International Context" also criticizes Negro leadership for supporting the Israelis and identifies Zionist interests with pro-Western neocolonialist, Zionist-oriented Jews such as the Rothschilds and the South African mining magnate, Harry F. Oppenheimer, in F. B. Barbour, ed., *The Black Power Revolt* [Boston: Extending Horizon Books, 1968].)

One of the perceptive analyses of the role of popular figures in this era is that of Claybourne Carson, Jr., ("Blacks and Jews in the Civil Rights Movement" in Washington, *Jews in Black Perspective*, 1984). Carson writes:

> Although SNCC's early leaders, often training for the Christian ministry, initially directed their appeals toward the Northern Christian student movement, SNCC's radicalization and the redirection of its fund-raising efforts each resulted from the entry into the group of Blacks who were products of this radical culture (of Black militancy) centered in New York. Thus the oft noted parallels between their Biblical stories of Jewish oppression and the travails of Afro-Americans were less significant in accounting for SNCC-Jewish ties than were the common experiences of a small minority of Afro-Americans and Jews: those whose attitudes were shaped by awareness of secular radicalism and political dissent, from labor organizing in the 1930's to more isolated protest activity in the 1940's and 1950's. (p. 116)

The irony of this development is that many of the popular public figures, especially Stokely Carmichael and Ron Karenga, learned the radicalism they would employ as Black Nationalists from Jewish socialists and other members of the Jewish Left. The roots of the anti-semitism Carmichael and Karenga displayed were to be found in a peculiar brand of Jewish secular political thought. SNCC's initial agenda was antibourgeois, a moralistic commitment to the cause of "oppressed people," rigorous African-American struggle as a necessary component of fundamental social change. Carmichael's election as head of SNCC in May 1966 marked the displacement of southern Black activist leadership (Carmichael replaced John Lewis, now a member of Congress) that was seen as too moderate, lacking in political sophistication, and insufficiently radicalized.

Finally, the contrasting viewpoints of two contemporary Black intellectuals will complete the survey of this genre of Black thought. Harold Cruse, *The Crisis of the Negro Intellectual* (New York: Morrow, 1967) argues that in the United States Negroes have yielded intellectual leadership to American Jews, thereby forfeiting the leadership of their own people. He calls for "Black assertiveness" and the elaboration of a Black "cultural nationalism" like that of the Jews as an answer to this problem (pp. 364, 497). Cruse debunks the idea of an "alliance" between Black and Jewish Americans and sees American Jews as traditionally noncommittal on slavery, abolition, segregation, and integration, except where their own rights were involved.

Frank Hercules, *American Society and Black Revolution* (New York: Harcourt, Brace, Jovanovich, 1972) on the other hand, insists that Christianity is a collateral ancestor of white racism (pp. 71–72), which has produced similar effects for both Jews and Black people. He cites Martin Luther King, Jr. for speaking glibly of the redemptive power of suffering "without, it seemed, overmuch thought for the possibility that the suffering he so nobly conceived might attain its ghastly culmination for blacks in American gas ovens and crematoria." Christian America, according to Hercules, is endemically racist, the spawn of Christian Europe (pp. 274–75, 362–89, 426–27). Therefore, Black anti-semitism, which he terms "a tiny rivulet of the giant watercourse of Western anti-semitism," is derived from white anti-semitism, "a Christian prejudice with which the converted Blacks have been infected." The remedy of this venomous anti-semitism, "actually more apparent than real," he says, is for Jews to make common cause with the Black underclasses in the class struggle.

> Black anti-semitism is in no sense ideological; it is a by-product, although deeply disturbing, of the black class struggle. . . . There lies the real danger of black anti-semitism: there, in the lower depths among the dispossessed. There is where black children catch the disease of anti-semitism, there in those horrible, festering, rotting slums. . . . On that level where poverty-stricken blacks confront Jewish merchants and landlords, genuine hatred is possible, and does in fact exist, against the Jew who is thought to be an exploiter and a bloodsucker, and this attitude does tend to spread across the whole group of Jewish people like ink spilled on blotting paper. (pp. 382–83)

As a concluding note, Black militancy is a widely encompassing term. It has been used frequently to include more moderate proponents of Black power (conceived of as political power at the polls) or even the pacifistic philosophy of Martin Luther King, Jr. In this essay, Black militancy is seen as a species of Black thought that has a particular relationship to the issue of Black anti-semitism. Wherever Black militancy has achieved an ideological formulation in which the notion of negritude has been elevated to a racist pitch, it has been accompanied by a distinct element of anti-semitism in the particular form of Jew-hatred. In such circumstances, disjointed elements of philosophical and poetic negritude, religious Ethiopianism, ghetto outrage, Pan-Africanism, and pro-

Arab anti-Zionism have become reified into a Kulturreligion of Black-ness with a particular dislike for Jews. Whether one dismisses Black militancy as the race adolescence of a segment of Black America coming of political and economic age or finds something hopeful in the greening of a root of Black American consciousness, one of its elements that remains especially troublesome is its blatant anti-semitism.

# Bibliography

Allport, Gordon. 1954. *The Nature of Prejudice.* Cambridge, Mass.: Addison-Wesley.

Baldwin, James. "The Harlem Ghetto." *Commentary* 5 (February).

———. 1955. *Notes of a Native Son.* Boston: Beacon.

———. 1967a. "Negroes are Anti-Semitic Because They're Anti-White." *New York Times Magazine,* 9 April.

———. 1967b. "Anti-Semitism and Black Power." *Freedomways* 7, no. 1 (Winter).

Bauer, Y. 1978. *The Holocaust in Historical Perspective.* Seattle: University of Washington Press.

Bayton, J. A. 1941. "Racial Stereotypes of Negro College Students." *Journal of Abnormal and Social Psychology* 36.

——— and Byoune, E. F. 1947. "Racio-National Stereotypes Held by Negroes." *Journal of Negro Education* 16.

Belth, Nathan C. 1979. *A Promise to Keep: A Narrative of the American Encounter with Anti-Semitism.* New York: Anti-Defamation League of B'nai B'rith.

Berson, Lenora E. 1971. *The Negroes and the Jews.* New York: Random House.

Bloom, Steven. 1973. *Interactions Between Blacks and Jews in New York City, 1900–1930 As Reflected in the Black Press.* New York University, unpublished doctoral dissertation.

Bontemps, Arna. 1974. "Black/Jewish Conflicts: The Fisk Consultation." *Christian Century* 91, no. 27 (31 July).

Brink, William and Louis Harris. 1963. *The Negro Revolution in America.* New York: Simon and Schuster.

Carr, E. H. 1961. *What is History.* New York: Random House.

Clark, Kenneth B. 1946. "Candor about Negro-Jewish Relations." *Commentary* 1, no. 2 (February).

———. 1957. "What Negroes Think About Jews." *ADL Bulletin* (December).

Cothran, Tilman C. 1951a. "Negro Conceptions of White People." *American Journal of Sociology* 56, no. 5 (March).

———. 1951b. "Negro Conceptions of White People in a Northeastern City." *American Journal of Sociology* (March).

Cruse, Harold. 1967. *The Crisis of the Negro Intellectual.* New York: Morrow.

Davis, Lenwood G. 1984. *Black-Jewish Relations in the United States, 1752–1984: A Selected Bibliography.* Westport, Conn.: Greenwood.

Diner, Hasai R. 1977. *In the Almost Promised Land: Jewish Leaders and Blacks, 1915–1935.* Westport, Conn.: Greenwood.

Dinnerstein, Leonard, ed. 1973. *Jews in the South.* Baton Rouge: Louisiana State University.

Drake, St. Clair, and Horace C. Cayton. 1945. *Black Metropolis*. New York: Harcourt, Brace.

Duker, Abraham G. 1965. "On Negro-Jewish Relations: A Contribution to a Discussion." *Jewish Social Studies* 27, no. 1 (January).

————. 1969. "Negroes versus Jews I: Anti-Semitism is Asserted." *Patterns of Prejudice* 3, no. 2 (March/April).

Evans, Eli N. 1973. *The Provincials: A Personal History of Jews in the South*. New York: Atheneum. esp. pp. 291–326, "Jews and Blacks."

Fast, Howard, in Shlomo Katz, ed. 1967. *Negroes and Jews: An Encounter in America*. New York: Macmillan.

Feuerlicht, Roberta Strauss. 1983. "The Fate of the Jews: A People Torn Between Israeli Power and Jewish Ethics." New York: Times Books.

Foner, Philip S. 1975. "Black-Jewish Relations in the Opening Years of the Twentieth Century." *Phylon* 36 (December).

Forster, Arnold and Benjamin R. Epstein. 1974. *The New Anti-Semitism*. New York: McGraw-Hill.

Frazier, E. F. 1963. *The Negro Church in America*. New York: Schocken Books.

Friedman, Murray. 1979. "Black Anti-Semitism on the Rise." *Commentary* 68, no. 4 (October).

Gans, Herbert J. 1969. "Negro-Jewish Conflict in New York." In Peter I. Rose, ed., *The Ethnic Experience and the Racial Crisis*. New York: Random House, 1972). Reprint from *Midstream* (March).

Glock, Charles Y., Gertrude J. Selznich, and Joe L. Spaeth. 1966. *The Apathetic Majority: A Study Based on Public Responses to an Eichmann Trial*. New York: Harper and Row.

Glock, Charles Y., and Ellen Siegelman, eds. 1969. *Prejudice U.S.A.* New York: Praeger.

Glock, Charles Y., and Rodney Stark. 1966. *Christian Beliefs and Anti-Semitism*. New York: Harper and Row.

Goldman, Peter. 1969. *Report from Black America*. New York: Simon and Schuster.

Halpern, Ben. 1971. *Jews and Blacks: The Classical American Minorities*. New York: Herder and Herder.

Harris, Louis, and Bert E. Swanson. 1970. *Black-Jewish Relations in New York City*. New York: Praeger.

Hellwig, David. 1973. "The Afro-American and the Immigrant" Syracuse University, unpublished doctoral dissertation.

Hertzberg, Stephen. 1978. *Strangers within the Gate City: The Jews of Atlanta, 1845–1915*. Philadelphia: Jewish Publication Society of America.

Hofstadter, R. *The Age of Reform*. New York: Vintage Books.

Jones, LeRoi. 1969. *Raise Rays Raze: Essays Since 1965*. New York: Random House.

————. and Neal, Larry. 1966. *Black Fire: An Anthology of Afro-American Writing*. New York: Morrow.

Karenga, Maulana Ron. 1966. *The Quotable Karenga*. Edited by Clyde Halisi and James Mtume. Los Angeles: n.p.

Labovitz, Sherman. 1975. *Attitudes Toward Blacks Among Jews: Historical Antecedents and Current Concerns*. San Francisco: R & E Research Associates.

Lenski, Gerhard. 1961. *The Religious Factor: A Sociological Study of Religion's Impact on Politics, Economics and Family Life.* Garden City, N.Y.: Doubleday.

Lester, Julius. 1979. "Confessions of a Former Anti-Semite." *The Village Voice* (10 September).

Littell, Franklin H. 1975. *The Crucifixion of the Jews.* New York: Harper and Row.

Martire, Gregory, and Ruth Clark. 1982. *Anti-Semitism in the United States: A Study of Prejudice in the 1980's.* New York: Praeger.

Marx, Gary T. 1967. *Protest and Prejudice: A Study of Belief in the Black Community.* New York: Harper and Row.

———. 1968. "Facts and Fallacies: Negro Anti-Semitism." *Nation* 206/1 (11 January).

Middleton, Russell. 1973. "Do Christian Beliefs Cause Anti-Semitism?" *American Sociological Review* 38 (February).

Neumann, Franz. 1944. *Behemoth: The Structure and Practice of National Socialism, 1933–1944.* New York: Harper and Row.

Owen, Chandler. 1942. "Negro Anti-Semitism: Cause and Cure." *National Jewish Weekly* 57, no. 1 (September).

Prothro, E. Terry, and John A. Jensen. 1952. "Comparison of Some Ethnic and Religious Attitudes of Negro and White College Students in the Deep South." *Social Forces* (May).

———. 1950. "Group Differences in Ethnic Attitudes of Louisiana College Students." *Sociology and Social Research* 34.

Quinley, Harold E., and Charles Y. Glock. 1979. *Anti-Semitism in America.* New York: Free Press/Macmillan.

Reddick, Lawrence D. 1942. "Anti-Semitism among Negroes." *Negro Quarterly* 1, no. 2 (Summer).

Ribuffo, L. P. 1983. *The Old Christian Right.* Philadelphia: Temple University Press.

Richardson, Ben. 1944. "Anti-Semitism and the Negro." *The Protestant* 5, no. 9 (June).

———. "No Anti-Semitism (by Negroes): This is Our Common Destiny." *People's Voice* (7 August).

Roof, Wade C. 1975. "Religious Orthodoxy and Minority Prejudice: Causal Relationship or Reflection of Localistic World View?" *American Journal of Sociology* 80, no. 3.

Rose, Peter I. 1983. *Mainstream and Margins: Jews, Blacks and Other Americans.* New Brunswick, N.J.: Transaction.

Schuman, Howard, and Shirley Hatchett. 1974. *Black Racial Attitudes: Trends and Complexities.* Ann Arbor: University of Michigan.

Selznick, Gertrude J., and Stephen Steinberg. 1969. *The Tenacity of Prejudice: Anti-Semitism in Contemporary America.* New York: Harper and Row.

Shankman, Arnold. 1979. "Friend or Foe? Southern Blacks View the Jews: 1880–1935." In *Turn to the South: Essays on Southern Jewry,* ed. Nathan M. Kaganoff, and Melvin I. Urofsky, Charlottesville: University Press of Virginia.

Sheppard, Harold L. 1947. "The Negro Merchant: A Study of Negro Anti-Semitism." *American Journal of Sociology* 53, no. 2 (September).

Simpson, George E., and Milton J. Yinger. 1953. *Racial and Cultural Minorities.* New York: Harper.

Sobel, B. Z., and Mae L. Sobel. 1966. "Negroes and Jews, Minority Groups in Conflict." *Judaism* 15 (Winter).

Stemons, James S. 1941. *As Victim to Victims: An American Negro Laments with Jews.* New York: Fortuny's.

Teller, Judd L. 1966. "Negroes and Jews: A Hard Look." *Conservative Judaism* 21, no. 5 (Fall).

———. "Jews and Blacks: Together." *National Jewish Monthly* 84 (January).

Tsukashima, Ronald T. 1978. *The Social and Psychological Correlates of Black Anti-Semitism.* San Francisco: R & E Research Associates.

———. 1979. "Black Anti-Semitism: A Test of Competing Hypotheses." Society for the Study of Social Problems, association paper.

———. and Darrell M. Montero. 1976. "The Contact Hypothesis: Social and Economic Contact and Generational Changes in the Study of Black Anti-Semitism." *Social Forces* 55, no. 1.

Washington, Joseph R. Jr. 1984. *Jews in Black Perspectives: A Dialogue.* Madison, N.J.: Fairleigh Dickenson University Press.

Wedlock, Lunabelle. 1942. *The Reaction of Negro Publications and Organizations to German Anti-Semitism.* The Howard University Studies in the Social Sciences, III/2. Washington, D.C.: Howard University.

Weisbord, Robert C., and Arthur Stein. 1970. *Bittersweet Encounter: The Afro-American and the American Jew.* Westport, Conn.: Negro Universities Press.

Whitfield, Stephen J. 1987. "A Critique of Leonard Dinnerstein's 'The Origins of Black Anti-semitism in America'." *American Jewish Archives,* vol. XXXIX (November) No. 2.

Wilkins, Roy. 1977. "Jewish-Negro Relations: An Evaluation." *Crisis* 86, no. 4 (June-July).

Wolf, Eleanor et al. 1944. *Negro-Jewish Relationships.* Detroit: Wayne State University Studies in Inter-Group Conflicts in Detroit.

Wright, Richard. 1937. *Black Boy: A Record of Childhood and Youth.* New York: Harper.

# Name Index

# Subject Index

137